D0460712

The Christmas Stocking Book

Mary D'Alton

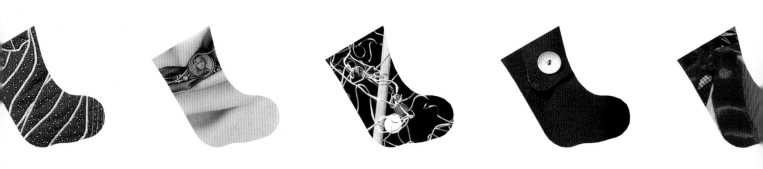

The Christmas Stocking Book

50 Exquisite Designs to Celebrate the Season

Mary D'Alton

Photography by
Eric Ferguson

Lark Books

Dedication

This book is dedicated to my family, with whom I have shared so many Christmases—
especially to my parents, who have lovingly filled so many Christmas stockings.

Editor: Laura Dover Doran
Art Direction/Production: Elaine Thompson
Photography: Eric Ferguson
Illustrations: Donlynna Peterson (pages 15 and 21) and Bobby Gold (elsewhere)
Proofreader: Julie Brown

Library of Congress Cataloging-in-Publication Data
D'Alton, Mary, 1962-
    The Christmas stocking book : 50 exquisite designs to celebrate the season/
Mary D'Alton. -- 1st ed.
        p.   cm.
    Includes index.
    ISBN 1-57990-050-X
    1. Christmas decorations.   2. Handicraft.   I. Title.
TT900.C4D35   1998
745.594'12--dc21   97-44118
                                                            CIP

10 9 8 7 6 5 4 3 2 1

First Edition

Published by Lark Books
50 College St.
Asheville, NC 28801, USA

© 1998, Mary D'Alton

Distributed by Random House, Inc., in the United States, Canada,
    the United Kingdom, Europe, and Asia

Distributed in Australia by Capricorn Link (Australia) Pty Ltd.,
    P.O. Box 6651, Baulkham Hills Business Centre, NSW 2153, Australia

Distributed in New Zealand by Tandem Press Ltd., 2 Rugby Rd.,
    Birkenhead, Auckland, New Zealand

The written instructions, photographs, designs, patterns, and projects in
this volume are intended for the personal use of the reader and may be
reproduced for that purpose only. Any other use, especially commercial use,
is forbidden under law without written permission of the copyright holder.

Every effort has been made to ensure that all the information in this book
is accurate. However, due to differing conditions, tools, and individual skills,
the publisher cannot be responsible for any injuries, losses, or other damages
that may result from the use of the information in this book.

Printed in Hong Kong

All rights reserved

ISBN 1-57990-050-X

Contents

Acknowledgments

I would like to wholeheartedly thank all the people who helped me put this book together, especially the following:

⬦

ERIC FERGUSON, photographer and stylist extraordinaire, who made this book so beautiful;

KAREN TIMM, for her enthusiasm and continuous support;

GEORGENE POMPLUN, for her optimism and encouragement;

DEB OPYD, for finding me the perfect tablecloth;

CAROL PORTER, for sharing her button collection;

CAROL BEAVER, for sharing her linens;

JOYCE ABERNATHY, for making the quilted stockings;

CAROLYN KALLENBORN, for her beautiful hand-dyed fabrics;

GRETCHEN NUTT, for her ribbon embroidery talent, and supply of antique and hand-dyed ribbon (from her store, Floriligium, in Madison, Wisconsin);

CAROL JAMESON, for her supply of antique trims (photographed in the window of her store, Old Time Shoppe, in McGregor, Iowa: see page 11);

MARGORIE FORD, for her handwoven fabrics;

PAM D'ALTON, my sister, for ideas, stitchery, and her endless supply of props;

ANNA CARLSON, for all of her support; and

thanks to my mom and dad.

Also, special thanks to DOROTHY BOND (Cottage Grove, Oregon), who allowed us to use the illustrations on pages 15 and 21.

Introduction

Stockings are a joy to make for a number of reasons. First, the possibilities in size, shape, and materials are endless, as is the array of gifts they can contain. The ideas were abundant for this book, with inspirations coming from a variety of sources: wonderful old fabrics and trims in antiques stores, memories of gifts received at past holidays, my children's drawings, and pieces of ribbon that came tied on gifts, to name only a few.

Stockings can be so simple that several can be constructed in an hour, or so complex that they require weeks of labor. They can be extremely personal, not only in what they're filled with but in

the way they are decorated. You can make them to give as memorable gifts, as heirlooms that will be used for many Christmases to come, or as simple decorations to celebrate the holiday season.

The stockings in this book are intended to be either duplicated exactly or to be used as a springboard for your own imagination. Get inspired. Take these ideas and add your own holiday memories and sentimental souvenirs. Add your favorite fabric, that button from your grandmother's gown, or fabric from a child's favorite blanket. Fill your stockings with treasures until they overflow and give them to your dearest friends and family. Have fun!

Materials and Supplies

T he importance of using high-quality
materials cannot be overestimated.
The materials you choose will not only
affect appearance, but will determine how long
the stocking will last. Don't limit yourself. Learn
to look at potential materials in a different way.
Pay attention at antique stores, flea markets, and
garage sales. Some of my best finds (and, thus,
my favorite stockings) have come unexpectedly.

Fabric

Probably the most crucial ingredient in a Christmas
stocking is fabric. Virtually any fabric can be used.
High-quality fabrics are more expensive, but usually
only a small piece is needed. Velvet, wool, wool felt,
boiled wool, synthetic fleece, sheer taffetas, shiny
satins, cut velvet, printed velvet, silk shantung, plaid
wools, cotton prints, and brocades are only a few of
the wonderful materials you have to choose from.
Many of the stockings in this book are in some form
of wool; wool hangs beautifully, is easy to work with,
comes in gorgeous colors, and looks warm and cozy.
You will also need wool bat or wool roving (loose-
weave fibers) for felt making.

A wide selection of fabric can usually be found at fabric stores and quilting shops. But don't limit yourself to a mediocre fabric or craft store. Fabric is everywhere in our daily lives—in our clothing, bedding, table linens, upholstery, drapes and curtains, and so forth. Fabric items that you think are useless may actually be perfect materials for a stocking or, at least, a cuff. And stockings made from cherished fabrics have added value. There are stockings in this book made from tablecloths (pages 45 and 84), fragments of old quilts (pages 24 and 40), kimonos from secondhand stores (pages 48 and 76), and even a hunting coat from a garage sale (page 53).

When choosing fabric, remember that, though all stockings look great filled with presents, if you want to hang a stocking empty (just for decoration), you will need a fabric with some body or a substantial lining fabric. Using wool, velvet, and other sturdy fabrics for stockings also allows the stockings to be hung full of goodies without stretching out of shape.

Basic Sewing Supplies

> Straight pins

> Sewing and embroidery needles in assorted sizes

> Scissors: high-quality, sharp fabric shears, as well as a pair of small scissors. Curved embroidery scissors are helpful for evening up fringe on the bottom edge of a tassel and for other small snips.

> A steam iron for pressing fabric, especially hems and seams

> Rotary cutter, mat, and cutting wheels

> A sewing machine is extremely helpful, but a necessity only when machine quilting.

Other Supplies

> Knitting yarns for making tassels (see page 14): cotton, wool, synthetic, or any combination

> Wool bat or wool roving for felt making

> Embroidery floss, both solid and variegated. You can also take strands of different-colored flosses and twist them together to create unique combinations of color and texture.

> Silk ribbon for ribbon embroidery

> Tea for dying ribbon to create subtle color changes (see pages 32 and 34). To do this, make a cup of tea,

cut lengths of silk ribbon, and put them in the tea to absorb the color. Most teas will darken any color and provide a rich hue. Some herbal teas with red colors create gorgeous shades of pink on white or cream-colored silk. The longer the ribbon sits in the tea, the darker the color will become. When the desired color is achieved, remove silk from tea and let dry. Press with an iron to set color.

- Assorted buttons, beads, and charms (see page 9)
- Chicken wire and various other wires in different colors, such as telephone wire
- Wood and other materials for nontraditional stockings (willow, grapevines, moss, and birch bark)
- Assorted ribbon (see below)

Ribbon

Ribbon is a passion of mine. Though you can find an assortment of ribbons at fabric stores and craft stores, I find the most unusual and beautiful pieces at floral shops, gift shops, antique stores, and flea markets. The variety of ribbon out there is amazing; it comes in widths from ⅛ inch (.3 cm) to 6 inches (15 cm); it can be plain, patterned, textured, smooth, and can have wired edges. Some ribbon is thin and sheer, some heavy and thick, and some a combination of both.

When choosing a ribbon, consider how each behaves best. Will it tie into a wonderful bow? Does it drape gracefully or catch and reflect the light when you twist it and stitch it down? Ribbon can have a lot of personality, and it can affect the design tremendously. Consider it carefully and don't just add it as an afterthought.

Don't make a stocking, then go out and search for the perfect ribbon. Chances are, you won't find it. I prefer to buy ribbon when I see it and keep it in baskets or draped over things in my studio for inspiration. Then, when I start planning a stocking, I usually have the ribbon I need within reach.

I have found some of my most beautiful ribbon in antiques stores. Often there is just a few yards wound on a piece of cardboard, and since most stockings require less than a yard of fabric, this is usually enough. In many cases antiques-store ribbon is a much higher quality than new ribbon and is often less expensive. Occasionally, I happen upon a store that has an abundance of old trims and ribbons, and I wish I could bring them all home with me. Make sure old trims and ribbons are in good condition. Sometimes light and time have broken down the fibers, and they will crack and break.

Developing a Design

When I begin to make a stocking, I've usually been inspired by one of the elements in the stocking: ribbon, fabric, a button, or a bead. I begin with this element, then sort through the baskets, boxes, jars, and piles of things around me to find other things that work with this element.

Once I have an interesting combination, I evaluate the fabric. The type of fabric can dictate the shape and size of the stocking, and that can affect ribbon size and the number of buttons or beads you will use. Keep in mind that the heavier, thicker fabrics make large stockings and don't work as well for small, graceful, or skinny stockings. Save the lighter-weight fabrics for those.

Once you've chosen the size and shape of the stocking, you can look at the trimmings that go with the fabric and see how they can be used. Do you have enough ribbon for a nice bow? Or is it a short, wide piece that would look better stitched to the top as a cuff? Do you have enough beads to cover the surface of a small stocking? Or one antique button that you want to feature?

Basic Stocking Construction

Refer to this section for instructions on how to construct a basic stocking, then follow instructions for individual stocking styles.

Note that all of the stocking patterns are found in the back of the book (see page 116). To use the patterns in the book, enlarge them on a photocopier (percentages are given) and cut around the shape. Pin the pattern to the fabric and cut around the pattern.

You will need two pieces of fabric for most stockings: one for the back and one for the front. If you are using one-sided fabric (fabric with a definite right and wrong side), be sure to cut a front piece and a back piece. This will prevent ending up with two front or back pieces, which wastes fabric.

METHOD #1

Most of the stockings in this book are constructed using this technique. Once your stocking pieces are cut

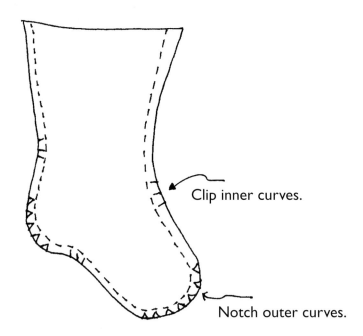

Clip inner curves.

Notch outer curves.

(see page 12), pin them with right sides together. Sew the pieces together, using a ¼-inch (.5-cm) seam allowance. (This seam allowance has been used in all of the patterns.)

With very sharp scissors, clip the inner curves and notch the outer curves as shown in the illustration. Turn the stocking right side out and press. If the fabric ravels easily, consider finishing the seams, perhaps by zigzagging.

METHOD #2

When working with fabrics that don't ravel, you can construct the pieces with wrong sides together and the seam allowance on the outside. This is a very simple and quick way to make stockings. To do this with a sewing machine, pin the stocking pieces with wrong sides together, stitch ¼ inch (.5 cm) from the edge, then trim the seam allowances evenly and close to the stitching (⅛ inch or .3 cm).

To finish by hand, baste the stocking pieces together (wrong sides together) and trim the edges so they are even. Then use a decorative embroidery stitch (usually a blanket stitch: see page 15) around the edges in a contrasting color of thread. In this way, the seam becomes part of the stocking design.

Lining

Though I don't give instructions for lining with most stockings in the book, I highly recommend lining stockings, as it improves the appearance of the stocking greatly. The fabric you choose for lining can also add character.

To line a stocking, simply use the pattern to cut an identical stocking from the lining fabric and sew the pieces together in the same way you would a stocking. There's no need to clip seams, because this stocking will not need to be turned.

Sew the liner stocking to the top edge of the outer stocking with right sides together, leaving about a 3-inch (7.5-cm) opening at the back edge. When you've finished stitching, push the lining to the inside of the stocking and stitch the opening closed by hand. You can also add a loop and stitch it to the inside of the stocking when you finish stitching up the lining.

Loops

Loops are easy to add to stockings. They can be made from a length of ribbon or trim; usually a 7-inch (18-cm) piece works well. If you want to make a loop from fabric, cut a piece of fabric 7 x 3 inches (18 x 7.5 cm), press the long sides in ⅞ inch (2.2 cm) so the sides overlap, and stitch the sides together by hand. Fold this long strip in half and stitch the two ends to the inside of the stocking. Remember that the loop has to be anchored very well if it's going to hold a heavy stocking.

Making Simple Tassels

Tassels are easy to make and are a nice addition to many stockings. Don't limit yourself to using only one type of yarn or thread in your tassels; combining two or more yarns or using a variegated yarn can create wonderful results.

Start by selecting the material you want to work with; make sure you have plenty so that the tassel will be full. Cut a piece of heavy paper or cardboard ⅛ inch (.3 cm) longer than the desired finished length of the tassel. Wrap the yarn around the cardboard until you have a thick layer of yarn. (This can vary anywhere from 10 times to 80 times around.)

Cut another piece out of the same yarn about 6 inches (15 cm) long, loop it through the top of the tassel, and tie a knot. Remove the tassel from the cardboard by sliding it off the end, wrap another piece of yarn around the tassel, and tie securely to keep the yarn

from slipping out. To finish, cut through the lower loop and trim the bottom ends with very sharp scissors until they are even. (Trimming sounds simple, but it's really important to be precise, so that the tassel doesn't look shaggy.)

Basic Stitches

Blanket Stitch

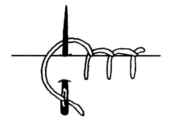

Come up through fabric about ¼ inch (.5 cm) in from the edge. Holding the thread with your thumb, go down and back up through fabric, bringing the needle under the thread and pulling the stitch into place.

Chain Stitch

Come up through fabric and shape the ribbon into a loop. Go back down and up again through fabric as shown, bringing the needle over the ribbon. Pull until the loop is the desired size. To end, take the needle down over the end of the last loop.

Rosette

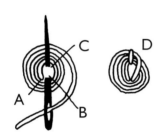

Come up at A. Go down at B and up at C. Wrap the thread around your needle three times, and, on the third time, pull the needle through B and up and out of C. Go down at D. Tack where necessary.

Backstitch

Bring the needle up from the back side of the fabric and go down through fabric to complete one stitch. Emerge from fabric and go back down for another stitch. As you work, move the needle ahead under the fabric and come up one stitch length again.

French Knot

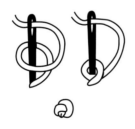

Bring needle out of fabric, wrap ribbon once or twice around needle. With needle flat against the fabric, rotate needle halfway around and insert it close to the starting point.

Cross Stitch

Make parallel straight stitches as shown, then reverse with parallel straight stitches to create crosses.

Note: Illustrations for blanket stitch, rosette, chain stitch, and cross stitch were created by Donlynna Peterson for *Embroidery Stitches from Old American Quilts* by Dorothy Bond.

Classic Stockings

ABCs and Trees
Stocking

I was fortunate enough to acquire some scraps from Marjorie Ford's studio; she's a talented weaver who works in Minneapolis, Minnesota.

I used her fabric as a base for this small cross-stitch sampler. For added interest, I raveled the edges of the cross-stitch fabric, then decided to ravel the edges of the woven fabric as well. If you don't have access to handwoven fabric, any loosely woven fabric will work fine.

YOU WILL NEED

Pattern #1 (see page 116)

Cross-stitch pattern (at right)

½ yard (.5 m) woven fabric

4-inch-square (10-cm) piece of cross-stitch fabric (linen), 30 threads per 1 inch (2.5 cm)

Cotton embroidery floss, variegated red and green, solid green, and tan

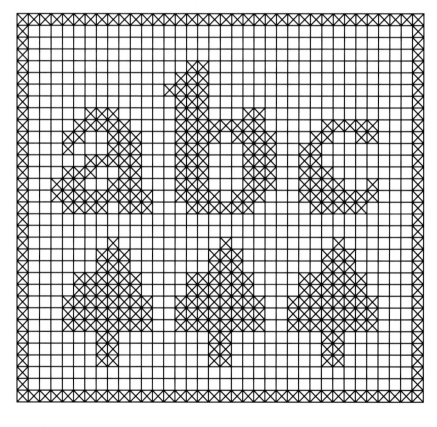

INSTRUCTIONS

Begin by using the pattern provided to work the cross-stitch design on the fabric; use the variegated floss for the ABC pattern, the green floss for the trees, and the tan floss for the trunks of the trees. When the basic design is complete, stitch the border with the variegated floss. Finish the stitching by trimming the fabric to ½ inch (1.5 cm) larger than the stitched border and unraveling the outer threads to create a fringe.

Sew the stocking together as described on page 13 (method #2) with the seam allowance on the right side, and unravel the fabric to achieve fuzzy edges. Stitch a 3- x 12-inch (7.5- x 30.5-cm) strip of fabric to the top for a cuff; unravel the edge of this piece as well. Position the cross-stitch sampler on the front of the stocking and stitch it in place.

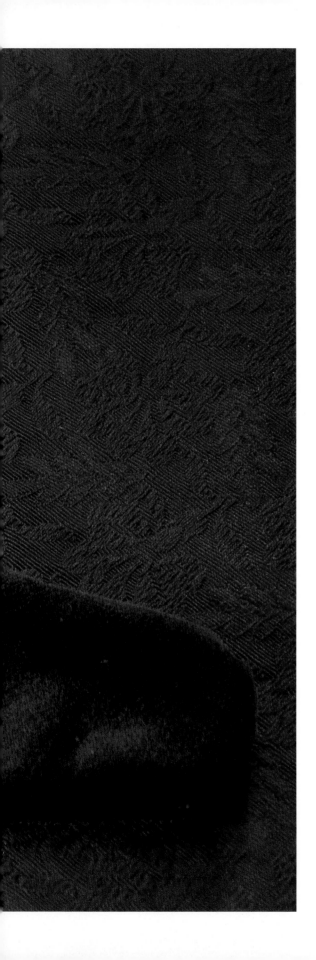

Black Velvet
Stocking

This stocking is 5½ inches (14 cm) tall and is almost small enough to hang on a Christmas tree as an ornament. Stitch someone's name or a holiday greeting with gold embroidery at the cuff and use this stocking to present a small gift.

YOU WILL NEED

Pattern #2 (see page 116)

¼ yard (.2 m) black velveteen

Gold thread or embroidery floss

1 yard (.9 m) gold braid (for loop)

2 gold tassels (see page 14)

INSTRUCTIONS

Using the pattern, cut two stocking pieces and construct the stocking as described on page 12 (method #1). Trim seams, turn right side out, and press. Hem top edge with a ¾-inch (2-cm) hem.

To make the cuff, cut a piece of the velveteen to 3½ x 7½ inches (9 x 19 cm) and sew the long edges together. Sew the short edges together to form a doughnut-shaped piece that fits around the upper edge of the stocking.

Embroider the cuff with gold thread: Make small, straight stitches and cross stitches (see page 15), then stitch several gold beads in the centers of the patterns. You can also stitch someone's name on the cuff at this point. Pin the cuff to the top edge of the stocking and stitch in place by hand.

Cut a 7-inch (18-cm) piece of gold braid for the hanger. If you want a thicker loop, do as I have done here: braid three strands of the braid together, knot the ends, and use this thick braid for the loop. Finally, make a pair of tassels (see instructions on page 14) and stitch the tassels to the base of the loop inside the cuff.

Boiled-Wool
Stocking

Embellishing with beads and embroidery will add a touch of elegance to any project. This boiled-wool stocking is blanket-stitched with silk thread and embroidered with a simple row of stitching. Although the band of embroidery seems complicated, it is really quite simple.

YOU WILL NEED

Pattern #3 (see page 116)

Embroidery design (below)

¼ yard (.2 m) ivory-colored boiled wool

Tiny glass beads, green

Embroidery floss: tan, brown, green, deep red, and gold. (On this stocking, the tan and the green are silk and the brown and the red are cotton, but any combination or all cotton would work fine.)

Narrow ribbon (optional)

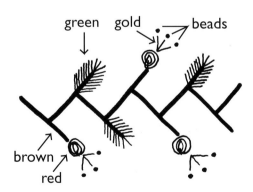

INSTRUCTIONS

To begin, cut the stocking pieces from the fabric according to the pattern and make a line with chalk on which to center your embroidery; this is especially important if you want to embroider on both front and back (so the design will match).

I started 2½ inches (6.5 cm) from the top edge of the stocking. Use the illustration provided to plan your design; if necessary, lightly transfer the design to the stocking with a fabric pen. Begin with the brown embroidery floss (straight stitches), then add stitches with green floss to simulate pine needles. Next, sew on red rosettes (see page 15), tiny gold stitches, and finish by adding the green beads.

When the embroidery is finished, construct the stocking. Baste the front and back pieces together by hand (method #2 on page 13). Trim the edges evenly. Then stitch over your basting, using the tan-colored thread and a blanket stitch (see page 15). To finish, stitch around the top opening of the stocking, again using a blanket stitch. Attach a narrow ribbon for a hanger, if desired.

Button
Stocking

For this stocking, I've chosen buttons in all one color, but you can certainly use any combination of your favorite buttons. I made the blue-and-white stocking for my mother as a Christmas gift. I was so pleased with the results, I decided to try it in green. You can dramatically change the look of this stocking simply by altering the colors of the wool and the buttons.

YOU WILL NEED

Pattern #1 (see page 116)

¼ yard (.2 m) white wool

7 or more buttons

Embroidery floss to match buttons

1 yard (.9 m) matching ribbon

Small beads (optional)

INSTRUCTIONS

Cut out the stocking pieces according to the pattern and determine which piece will be the front side. (Note that the top stocking is an exact pattern replication, and the one on the bottom has several inches added to its neck.) Position the buttons on the stocking and experiment with placement to create a pleasing arrangement. Once you are happy with the design, stitch the buttons in place.

Using embroidery floss, stitch around each button with rows of French knots (see page 15), small cross-stitches (see page 15), or simple straight lines, until you have filled the space and are pleased with the appearance. You can see from my stockings that you will not always be able to stitch all the way around a button without getting too close to another button; this adds to the interest of the pattern. If desired, add some small beads (in the same color) to the design with the embroidery floss.

Once the embroidery is complete, stitch the stocking together as described on page 12 (method #1), hem the top edge ¾ inch (2 cm), and make a loop (see page 13). Tie a bow in the ribbon and stitch it to the edge of the stocking.

HANGING STOCKINGS

Simple loops can be made easily out of the same fabric as the stocking, out of fabric in a contrasting color (see page 13), or with a length of ribbon. On the Crazy Quilt Stocking, I made a loop of ribbon and held it in place with a button (see page 25). In some cases—when you are hanging stockings on a stair rail, for example—a closed loop won't work; you'll need a hanger that will open and close. In this case, make a loop that buttons or snaps in place. Another option is to stitch the center of a long piece of ribbon to the stocking and simply tie a bow for a hanger (see pages 36 and 42).

Crazy Quilt
Stocking

I found this piece of crazy quilt in an antique store; someone had made it into a small purse. I fell in love with the fabric, but I didn't need the purse, so I found other uses for the quilt pieces. A variety of fabric scraps can be used as gorgeous stocking cuffs. The trick is to learn to see the potential in scraps at flea markets and antique stores and not to be afraid to create something around the piece.

YOU WILL NEED

Pattern #8 (see page 121)

A piece of fabric for the cuff,
18 x 7 inches (45.5 x 18 cm)

A piece of fabric for cuff lining,
18 x 7 inches (45.5 x 18 cm)

½ yard (.5 m) fabric for stocking
(in this case, black velvet)

Ribbon in a complementary color,
approximately 9 inches (23 cm)

Decorative button

INSTRUCTIONS

A stocking made from found materials requires that you begin with the chosen fabric, then decide how you will use the piece. If it's a scrap that's not large enough for a cuff, find another piece of fabric you can appliqué the scrap on.

Once you decide how the cuff will be made, construct the cuff. Cut lining fabric to the same size as you did the cuff fabric. Place cuff fabric right sides together with lining fabric, pin pieces together, and stitch the two long sides. Turn right side out and press. Now you have a long tube; stitch the ends of the tube together to form a doughnut shape.

Alter your stocking pattern to fit the cuff, if necessary. Construct the stocking by sewing the right sides together as described on page 12 (method #1) and finish the top edge with a ¾-inch (2-cm) hem. Pin the cuff in place and stitch.

Choose a sturdy ribbon for the hanger—not something that will stretch out of shape easily; here, I used black velvet. Loop the ribbon around and stitch it firmly to the stocking. Add the button over the stitching as shown in the photograph (above). To finish the stocking, trim the edges of the ribbon at a slant.

𝓕olk Art
Stocking

T he inspiration for this stocking was a hooked rug I saw at an auction. The rug featured circles surrounded by oak leaves and reminded me of felt folk art pieces I've seen with circles and blanket stitch. Then I realized the colors in the rug were similar to those in my pile of wool felt at home, and that adding blanket stitch to the pattern would make for a fun stocking.

YOU WILL NEED

Pattern #1 (see page 116)

Patterns for circles and leaves (below)

Wool felt: ¼ yard (.2 m) for the stocking, black; scraps of green, purple, cream, gold, light blue, and dark red for the design

Cotton embroidery floss: black, gold, dark red, and light blue

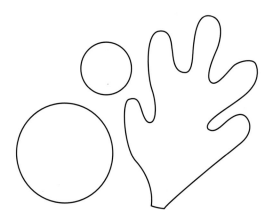

Enlarge 200%

INSTRUCTIONS

Using the patterns provided, cut the body of the stocking from black felt. Next, use the patterns on this page to cut three leaves (from green felt) and the circles. You will need four small circles (one black, two dark red, and one gold); four medium-sized circles (one each of purple, light blue, cream, and dark red); and four large circles (one each of gold, dark red, purple, and cream).

Using a blanket stitch (see page 15), stitch all around each of the three leaves. Stack the circles on each other as shown in the photograph. Again using a blanket stitch (with thread in a contrasting color), attach the circles to each other by stitching through two layers at once. When the circles have been connected, lay the pieces on the front piece of the stocking as shown and pin in place. Attach the pieces to the stocking with tiny, invisible stitches on the front of the felt.

Baste the stocking together around the edges as described on page 13 (method #2) and trim the edges evenly. Blanket-stitch the edges together on top of the basting stitch. Remove the basting. Finish by stitching a felt loop to the inside of the top of the stocking for a hanger.

YOU WILL NEED

Pattern #2
(see page 116)

¼ yard (.2 m)
burgundy velveteen

Approximately
9 inches (23 cm)
½-inch (1.5-cm) trim

Bee-shaped bead
or button

Tiny gold beads,
about 30

Gardener Stocking

Fill this adorable little stocking with seed packets, honey, and beeswax candles and present it to your favorite, anxious-for-spring gardener. The gold trim on this stocking is an antique-store find, but you can substitute any other ½-inch (1.5-cm) trim.

INSTRUCTIONS

Begin by constructing the stocking out of the velveteen: Cut two pieces from the pattern and sew the pieces together with right sides together as described on page 12 (method #1). Turn the stocking right side out. Finish the top edge with a zigzag machine stitch or an overcast stitch by hand to prevent raveling.

Press in ¾ inch (2 cm) on the top edge, but don't hem yet. Mark 1 inch (2.5 cm) down from the pressed top edge of the stocking and center the trim on that line. Pin, then stitch the trim in place. Stitch the tiny gold beads in a random pattern on the remaining space between the trim and the top edge. Stitch the hem in place. Finally, position the bee-shaped bead and stitch. If desired, add a loop so the stocking can be hung (see page 13).

Lace Collar
Stocking

I n another life, the lace on this stocking was a collar on a lady's dress. The front edge of the collar was torn, so I stitched it up and hid the repaired portion under the back of the stocking. Lace cuffs also make interesting tops for tiny stockings.

YOU WILL NEED

Pattern #1 (see page 116)

15-inch (38-cm) lace collar or piece of lace

½ yard (.5 m) pink wool felt

Cotton or silk embroidery floss

Small glass beads

INSTRUCTIONS

If you're working with an old collar or piece of lace, first measure what you have to work with; most likely, the pattern will need to be customized to fit the size of the collar. Here, I've used pattern #1 on page 116.

When you have cut the stocking pieces from the felt, stitch tiny stars all over the surface of the front of the stocking (or the front and the back, if you wish), using straight stitches. Then stitch beads in between the stars. (Be sure to leave enough room around the edges to sew the front and back stocking pieces together.)

Stitch the front to back with right sides together as described on page 12 (method #1), and trim and clip seams. Turn and steam press lightly. Pin the lace to the top edge of the stocking, then stitch in place to the inside of the stocking. Make a loop out of the felt and stitch the loop to the inside of the stocking.

Heirloom Stocking

C herished gifts deserve elegant enclosures. This stocking is the perfect container in which to pass a family heirloom from one generation to the next—and the stocking itself just may become an heirloom. It was designed to show off a Victorian button; an alternative would be to attach an antique brooch, charm, or locket to a ribbon and pin the ribbon to the stocking.

YOU WILL NEED

Pattern #2 (see page 116)

¼ yard (.2 m) black velvet

10 inches (25.5 cm) 1½-inch (4-cm) black, pleated ribbon

10 inches (25.5 cm) 2-inch (5-cm) magenta satin ribbon or ½ yard (.5 m) satin lining fabric

Decorative button

INSTRUCTIONS

Construct the stocking: Cut the pieces according to the pattern and stitch with right sides together as described on page 12 (method #1).

This stocking is not completely lined, but has a 2-inch (5-cm) satin ribbon stitched in as a facing. The ribbon has wired edges, which provides some body to the top of the stocking. Measure the magenta satin ribbon to fit the top edge of the stocking plus ½-inch (1.5-cm) seam allowance. Stitch the ends of the ribbon together to form a circle with a ¼-inch (.5-cm) seam allowance.

To finish the top edge of the stocking, stitch ribbon to the upper edge of the stocking with right sides together and fold ribbon to the inside.

Determine the placement of the black ribbon around the stocking and pin; the placement will, to some degree, depend on the size and shape of the button. Stitch the ribbon and button in place.

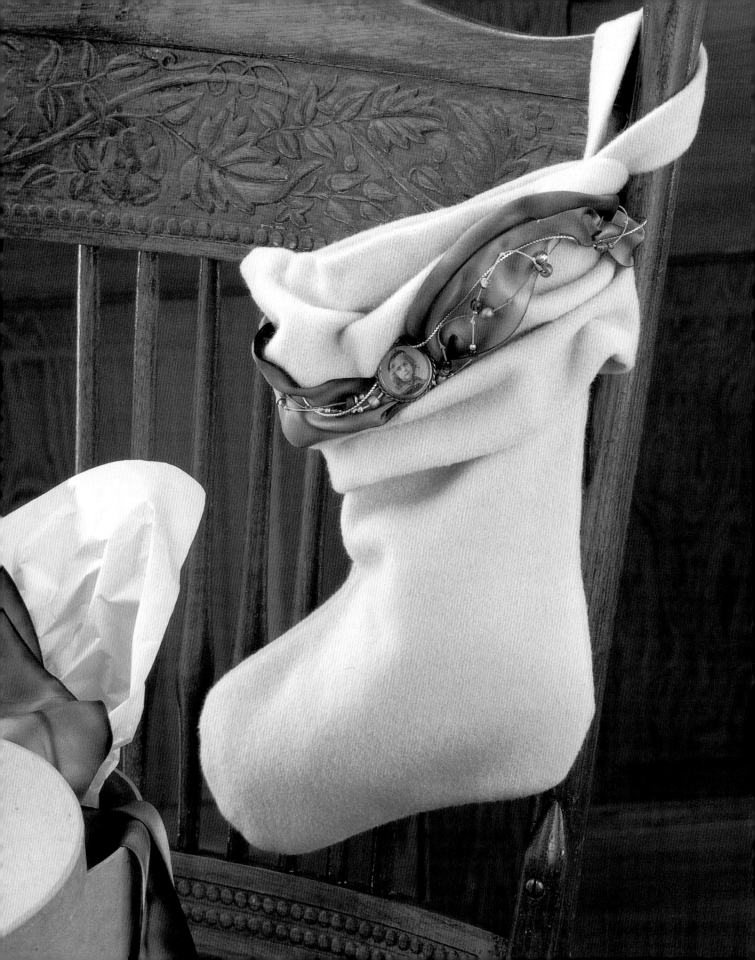

Photo Pin
Stocking

An antique photo pin is the focal point of this stocking; including an old photo of a family member makes a stocking a very meaningful gift. Any other antique brooch or pin can also be used. A variation would be to suggest a theme with the pin. For example, a teapot pin could adorn the cuff, and the stocking could be filled with a variety of herbal teas and a teacup.

YOU WILL NEED

Pattern #4 (see page 117)

½ yard (.5 m) cream-colored wool

½ yard (.5 m) 2-inch (5-cm) hand-dyed silk ribbon

½ yard (.5 m) ⅛-inch (.3-cm) gold braid

2 colors of waxed linen thread, 1 yard (.9 m) each

Assorted beads

INSTRUCTIONS

Construct the body of the stocking by using the pattern to cut two pieces and sewing the stocking together with right sides together as described on page 12 (method #1). Press in ¾ inch (2 cm) on the top of the stocking and hem.

Cut a piece of wool for the cuff, 20 x 8½ inches (51 x 21.5 cm). Stitch the short sides of the cuff pieces together and press the seam open. Press under ½ inch (1.5 cm) on the long sides, and sew a hem by hand so that the stitches don't show on the right side.

Place the cuff over the upper edge of the stocking; it will be quite a bit larger than the top of the stocking. Manipulate the cuff, scrunching it together all the way around the stocking, then secure with pins. With matching thread, stitch the cuff in place. This will take many small stitches.

Cut two long pieces of waxed linen, and string a random assortment of beads onto each piece. Every ½ inch (1.5 cm) or so, tie knots in the thread to create space between the beads and allow them to move along the thread freely.

Lay the ribbon over the cuff and place the linen threads and gold braid over the ribbon. Move the ribbon and the threads around until the pieces settle among the folds in the cuff. Secure the pin in place, pinning all the way through the ribbon and cuff.

With matching thread, tack everything in place. On the back of the cuff, tuck the ends of the ribbon and thread in between two wrinkles and stitch them in place so they are hidden. To finish, make a loop out of the cream-colored wool and attach to the inside of the stocking.

Woven Ribbon
Stocking

The subtle color variations of hand-dyed ribbon give this woven stocking a lovely, sumptuous feel. Because silk ribbon is quite delicate, it has been stitched to a felt backing to give the stocking more body. The narrow accent ribbon has wired edges, which makes it easy to manipulate. The ribbon is anchored to the stocking with tiny antique buttons.

YOU WILL NEED

Pattern #1 (see page 116)

2½ yards (2.3 m) 2½-inch-wide (6.5-cm) bias-cut, hand-dyed silk ribbon

¼ yard (.2 m) silk in a matching color (for the back piece)

¼ yard (.2 m) wool felt, as close to the color of the ribbon as possible

2 yards (1.8 m) ¼-inch (.5-cm) wired ribbon

6 or 7 antique buttons

INSTRUCTIONS

Using the pattern, cut two stocking pieces from the felt. The ribbon will be woven on top of one of these pieces. Cut ribbon into strips that cover the piece both lengthwise and crosswise, and carefully lay the ribbon strips over the felt. Be sure to leave some extra ribbon on the sides for the seam allowance—not too much, though, since silk ribbon is expensive.

You will need to pin the ribbon to the felt as you weave, but be careful to place the pins only at the edges of the ribbon or where another ribbon will be weaving over it;

in delicate ribbons, the pin holes may be permanent. Pin the vertical ribbons in place and weave the horizontal ones through them, gently shifting the design until you have covered all of the felt (see photograph). Baste the ribbons in place by hand.

Cut one stocking shape from the solid silk fabric and baste it to the other felt piece. Next, pin the front piece (ribbon basted to felt) to the back piece (silk basted to felt) and stitch the two pieces together as described on page 12 (method #1). Again, remember to be careful of the pins in the ribbon. Don't clip and notch into the seam allowance; just trim it off to leave only ⅛ inch (.3 cm).

Cut the piece of narrow ribbon in half, lay the two pieces on top of each other, fold them in half, and tie a knot in the ribbons about 2 inches (5 cm) from the fold to form a loop, a knot, and four trailing ends. Stitch the knot to the edge of the stocking. Twirl the four trailing ribbon ends around your finger and arrange the ribbon ends on the front of the stocking. Secure the pieces with the tiny buttons and trim off any excess ribbon.

Silk-Ribbon Embroidered
Stocking

The challenge in executing this splendid embroidered stocking is making sure the stitching in the back is neatly hidden behind the sheer gold ribbon. This can be frustrating, but can be completely remedied by choosing an opaque ribbon. Gretchen Nutt, who created this fabulous embroidery, is known for her needlework and dyes her own silk ribbon to give her stitchery added interest.

YOU WILL NEED

Pattern #5 (see page 118)

Embroidery pattern
(page 39)

½ yard (.5 m) velvet

18 inches (45.5 cm) 4-inch
(10 cm) metallic ribbon

Silk ribbon: green, pink,
and blue, ¼ inch wide
(.5 cm)

½ yard (.5 m) lining fabric
or 1 yard (.9 m) ribbon
for facing

At least 1 yard (.9 m)
silk ribbon for a bow

Decorative button

INSTRUCTIONS

The first step is embroidering the ribbon. If you choose to use sheer metallic ribbon, you won't have any trouble transferring the embroidery pattern onto the ribbon; simply place the pattern behind the ribbon and trace the design on the ribbon with a fabric marker.

Stitch the green portions of the pattern first. The trick is to remember that the ribbon is sheer and that the work on the back will be seen on the front. Gretchen used a series of stitches of different lengths to negotiate the curves. Make the leaves with chain stitches (see page 15). The pink flowers are French knots (see page 15) with straight stitches going out from the center, and the blue flowers are plain French knots. Sew the button on as the centerpiece.

Construct the velvet stocking as described on page 12 (method #1) and either line the stocking (see page 13) or put a narrow hem in the top edge. You can also finish the top edge with a ribbon facing with a 36-inch (91.5-cm)

(continued on page 39)

Enlarge 135%

(continued from page 37)

length of 1½-inch (4-cm) ribbon. Pin the edge of the ribbon to the top edge of the stocking with right sides together. Stitch with a ¼-inch (.5-cm) seam allowance. Fold the ribbon to the inside of the stocking and press. Tack the loose edge of ribbon in place.

Stitch the ends of the gold ribbon (on which you have embroidered) together to form a circle with a 16-inch (40.5-cm) circumference. Slip this circle over the top of the stocking until the top edge of the gold ribbon is 2 to 3 inches (5 to 7.5 cm) below the top edge of the stocking. (It won't be perfectly even all the way around, because of the curve in the top edge of the stocking.) Pin the ribbon in place. There will be more fabric than ribbon, so create small pleats in the fabric as you go. Pin pleats in place. Stitch the ribbon to the stocking by hand.

To finish this stocking, find the center of the piece of ribbon you have chosen for the hanger and stitch the center point to the upper edge of the stocking. Tie a bow with the ribbon to hang.

Quilt
Stocking

Because quilting is such an established sewing tradition, I felt I should include several quilted stockings in this book. Joyce Abernathy is a talented quilter from LaCrosse, Wisconsin, who continually impresses me with her work. This is one of Joyce's original designs. She often uses portions of quilts given to her by others who have begun, but never finished, quilting projects. What better way to preserve a piece of an old quilt than on a stocking?

YOU WILL NEED

    Pattern #9 (see page 122)

    Quilt scrap

    ½ yard (.5 m) fabric for body

    ½ yard (.5 m) muslin for backing

    ½ yard (.5 m) thin batting

INSTRUCTIONS

Use the pattern to cut out the stocking pieces. Cut the quilted piece to fit the top edge of your stocking and stitch in place to form a cuff on both the front and back piece of the stocking. Using the stocking pattern again, cut batting pieces and muslin backing. Sandwich the batting between the fabric and the muslin. Baste through all three layers (fabric, batting, and muslin) or use large safety pins to secure pieces.

For the stocking in the photograph, Joyce quilted the upper portion with her sewing machine, then added snowflakes over the lower portion of the stocking. Her sewing machine makes this decorative stitch, but you can also stitch the snowflakes by hand. See the instructions for making snowflakes on the Elf Boot Stocking on page 62.

To finish, stitch the front to the back of the stocking as described on page 12 (method #1) and sew a loop to the inside of the stocking. This stocking's loop was made from a quilt scrap.

CREATING STOCKING PATTERNS

More than once, I have gathered together stocking gifts and realized that everything would not fit in the chosen stocking. This situation calls for a pattern development technique that I encourage you to try—I have been quite satisfied with it. On a piece of newspaper or other paper, arrange the gifts that you wish to fill the stocking with, in as close to a stocking shape as you can manage. Draw around this shape on the paper, so that when you move the gifts, you have a rough stocking shape. Compare the stocking patterns you already have to this shape (possibly one in this book) and make the necessary adjustments, keeping in mind the depth may need to be altered to accommodate your gifts. It's this easy to create a customized stocking pattern.

Vintage Lace
Stocking

Stockings are a great way to showcase a favorite piece of lace. The lace on this stocking came with a tin of antique buttons I bought at a flea market. I had no idea it was there until I dumped out the tin to look through the buttons. This stocking would also look terrific filled with dried flowers and hung on a door or from a banister. For a friend who loves antique linens and lace, fill it with a pair of vintage embroidered pillowcases and some pretty soaps.

YOU WILL NEED

Pattern #4 (see page 117)

⅓ yard (.3 m) of neutral-colored wool

Lace, at least 20 inches (51 cm)—30 inches or 76 cm is ideal

Assorted shell buttons

2 yards (1.8 m) of cream-colored satin ribbon

INSTRUCTIONS

Cut two stocking pieces according to the pattern. Sew with right sides together and turn the stocking right side out as described on page 12 (method #1). Hem the top edge of the stocking with a ¾-inch (2-cm) hem. Pin the lace around the upper edge of the stocking. Gather or pleat as desired; this will depend on the length of lace. Stitch the lace in place along the top edge.

Arrange the shell buttons over the lace at the top and stitch buttons in place. (The number and size of buttons can be adjusted to fit the style of lace and the desired look.) Find the approximate center of the satin ribbon and pin center point to the inside of the stocking. Sew ribbon firmly in place. Last, tie the ribbon into a large bow.

STORING STOCKINGS

When the holiday season has past, and your stockings need to be packed away, put some effort into storing them properly. With a little extra care, your cherished handmade Christmas stockings will last a long time. The best way to preserve them is to stuff the stocking cavity with tissue, wrap the entire stocking in tissue, then tuck each stocking into its own box. Do not store them with other holiday decorations, as they are sure to get folded up or crushed. It is also important that you store stockings in a dry place; this helps keep the fabric and ribbon in good condition.

Tablecloth
Stocking

Since an antique tablecloth provided the linen to make this stocking, it seems appropriate to use it as part of a table setting. Indeed, it's a fun way to present silverware for a holiday meal. Place several mints in the toe of the stocking for an after-dinner treat.

YOU WILL NEED

Pattern #2 (see page 116)

Scrap of linen, 9 x 14 inches (23 x 35.5 cm)

10 inches (25.5 cm) narrow trim

About 1 skein each ¼-inch (.5-cm) silk ribbon, red and green

Several tiny gold beads

INSTRUCTIONS

Cut out the stocking pieces and decide where on the front piece the embroidery will go. Begin the silk-ribbon embroidery by making three or four rosebuds. To make a rosebud, cut a 1- to 1½-inch (2.5- to 4-cm) length of ribbon, roll up the ribbon, and stitch one end closed. Sew the rosebuds to the fabric with small stitches.

Once the rosebuds are in place, add some long and short stitches in between the roses with the green silk ribbon. Then stitch tiny buds with red ribbon by making French knots (see page 15) at the ends of the green stitches. Stitch gold beads into the design randomly.

When the embroidery is finished, construct the stocking as described on page 12 (method #1). Pin trim around upper edge of stocking and stitch in place by hand.

Red Holly
Stocking

Wool melton is a wonderful fabric for warm winter coats, and I discovered that you can appliqué it without finishing the edges. Because the fabric has been partially felted, it is slow to ravel. This stocking can also be made of felt, although wool gives it a richer surface.

YOU WILL NEED

Pattern #4 (see page 117)

Pattern for holly leaves and berries
(at right)

½ yard (.5 m) red wool melton

INSTRUCTIONS

Using the pattern provided, cut the stocking pieces out of the wool. Use the patterns on this page to cut out holly leaves and berries from the leftover wool scraps. Pin the leaves and berries in place on the front of the stocking (use the photograph as a guide) and sew the pieces in place with tiny stitches. I've found that using a thread that's a shade darker than the fabric color makes the stitches less noticeable on the surface of the wool.

Sew the stocking together as described on page 12 (method #1). Press in ¾ inch (2 cm) on the top edge of the stocking and hem. Cut three strips of wool, each about ½ x 10 inches (1.5 x 25.5 cm) and braid the strips together. Stitch each end of the braided cord and sew to the inside of the stocking to serve as a loop.

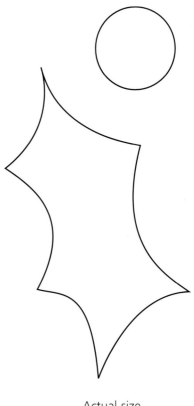

Actual size

Contemporary Stockings

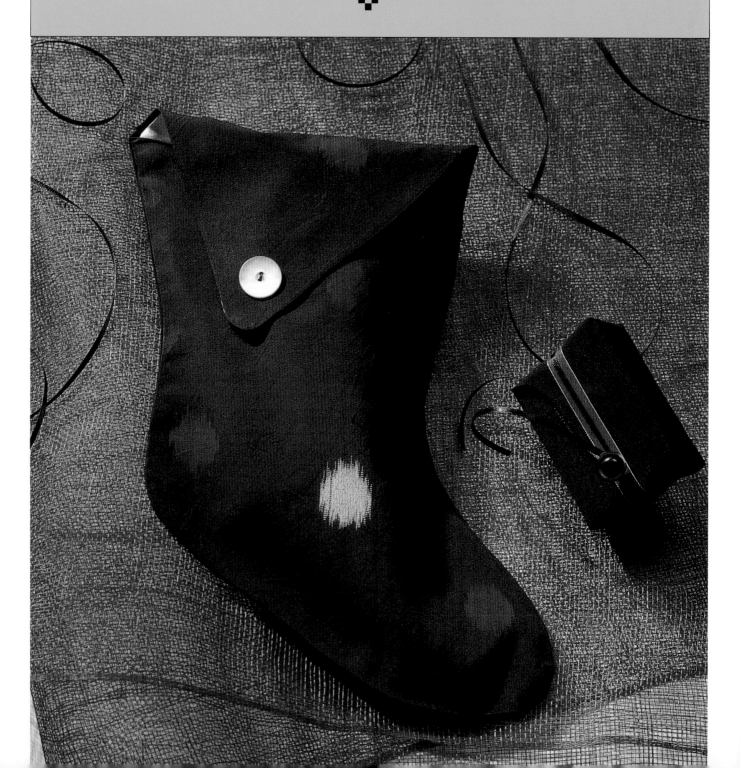

Envelope Kimono
Stocking

Believe it or not, the inspiration for this stocking *was* an envelope. The stocking was made from silk on a kimono that I found in the basement of a secondhand clothing store. I used the kimono's lining for the stocking lining. My choice of fabric creates a rather formal stocking, but a fun variation would be to make a stocking that imitates a Santa Claus hat: a stocking of red fabric with a white tassel stitched to the point of the flap.

YOU WILL NEED

Pattern #11 (see page 124: both front and back pieces)

½ yard (.5 m) each stocking fabric and lining fabric (or an old kimono)

Decorative button

INSTRUCTIONS

Cut the stocking pieces according to the pattern and construct the stocking as described on page 12 (method #1). Line the stocking as described on page 13. Before you join the stocking and the lining, put a row of reinforcing stitching ⅜ inch (1 cm) from the edge along the top edge of the front of the stocking (where there is a curve). Carefully clip up to, but not through, this line, along the length of the curve. This will make putting in the lining easier and everything will lie smoothly when the stocking is finished.

Stitch the lining to the stocking with right sides together, leaving a few inches (5 cm) on the side of the flap for turning. Turn and press. There are several different ways to deal with the closure: You may want to make a buttonhole in the flap and stitch a button on the stocking in the appropriate place. You can also place the button on the flap and stitch a snap under the flap to use as a closure.

Denim Star
Stocking

My sister collects all sorts of star-shaped things, so it seemed appropriate for her to make a star stocking. She took the face for the star from an old pot holder (from around the 1940s) that hangs in her kitchen.

Actual size

YOU WILL NEED

Pattern #1 (page 116)

Star pattern (at right)

Old, faded pair of jeans

2 circles of white muslin, each
4¼-inches (11.5-cm) diameter

¼ yard (.2 m) red cotton fabric

Cotton embroidery floss, red

Fabric pen or tailor's chalk

INSTRUCTIONS

Photocopy the design pattern provided and trace the star face onto one of the muslin circles. To trace the design on the fabric, place the design on top of the fabric and either put it on a light table or hold it up on a window with light coming through. Embroider the design using a backstitch (see page 15). Once the embroidery is complete, stitch the face to the other muslin circle with right sides together, leaving about 1½ inches (4.5 cm) open. Clip the seams, turn the circle right sides out (through the open section), and handstitch the opening closed.

Make the star in the same way as you did the circle and stitch the pieces right sides together with a ¼-inch (.5-cm) seam allowance. Clip the seams, turn right side out, and press. Stitch the circle to the star with red embroidery floss, about ¼ inch (.5 cm) from the outer edge.

Construct the stocking out of the denim: cut the pieces according to the pattern and sew the pieces together with right sides together as described on page 12 (method #1). Finish the top edge with a ¾-inch (2-cm) hem. Make a loop from a 10-inch (25.5-cm) piece of denim and stitch it to the corner of the stocking at an angle. Position the star on the stocking and stitch in place.

Buffalo Plaid
Stocking

Although quality wool is expensive, many garments have enough wool for a stocking or two. In this way, a Christmas stocking can give new life to a favorite piece of clothing or a blanket that you can't bear to throw out. The black-and-red plaid in this one was a hunting jacket I found at a garage sale; an old wool shirt also works.

YOU WILL NEED

Pattern #4 (see page 117)

Old jacket with a pocket and flap in good condition or any piece of plaid fabric, 6 x 20 inches (15 x 51 cm)

INSTRUCTIONS

When you lay out the pattern for this stocking, look at the fabric carefully before you begin to cut. On the jacket I used, I found that on the front where the pocket was stitched, the plaid of the jacket didn't match the plaid of the pocket, which really bothered me. So I cut out my stocking pieces, keeping in mind that I wanted to move the pocket and place it where the plaids matched. Remove the pocket with a seam ripper and stitch it back on the fabric so that the plaids line up. *Note:* If you do not have a pocket, you can easily construct one by sewing a square of plaid fabric to the front of the stocking.

Once the pocket is placed, the stocking can be constructed as described on page 12 (method #1). Make a loop with leftover scraps (see page 13) and attach loop to the inside of the stocking. Lightweight denim makes a wonderful lining for this stocking (see page 13 for lining instructions).

Black-and-Gold
Stocking

The cuff of this stocking is similar to a collage, with ribbon, beads, and holly leaves placed in a random fashion over two layers of fabric.

YOU WILL NEED

Pattern #4 (see page 117)

Pattern for the holly leaves (below)

½ yard (.5 m) black velvet

¼ yard (.2 m) gold lamé or a piece 6 x 20 inches (15 x 51 cm)

¼ yard (.2 m) sheer black fabric with metallic threads

1½ yard (1.4 m) ⅛-inch (.3-cm) black ribbon

1½ yard (1.4 m) ⅛-inch (.3-cm) gold braid

Gold beads in two sizes, ¼-inch (.5-cm) diameter and ⅛-inch (3-cm) diameter

Craft foam, ⅛ inch (.3 cm) thick

Gold acrylic paint

Craft knife

White craft glue

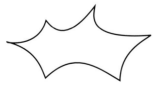

Actual size

INSTRUCTIONS

Begin by cutting the holly leaves from the foam and painting the leaves gold. (A sharp craft knife works better than scissors for cutting the foam.) It may take two coats of paint to get a nice, shiny surface. Cut a rectangle of gold lamé 6 x 20 inches (15 x 51 cm), stitch the long sides together, then stitch the short edges together to form a doughnut-shaped piece. Pinch the fabric randomly in spots, pin, and, with matching gold thread, stitch to keep the pinched fabric in place.

Next, make another doughnut-shaped piece with the black sheer fabric. When the cuff is complete, you should be able to see through one layer of fabric to the other. Stitch the short ends of the black sheer fabric together and place the gold cuff inside the black piece. Then wrap the long ends of the black fabric around the gold and sew the long ends together. Repeat the pinching and stitching process with the sheer fabric.

Tack one end of the black ribbon to the center back of the cuff (where the seam is) and arrange the ribbon on the surface of the fabric, tacking it in place with a needle and thread as you go. Use as much ribbon as needed and cut off any extra. Repeat this process with the gold braid.

Stitch the largest beads in place on the surface of the cuff in groups of three; try to imitate the appearance of holly berries. Stitch smaller beads randomly to the cuff. Glue the foam holly leaves in place.

Construct the black velvet stocking by sewing right sides together as described on page 12 (method #1). Finish the top edge with a ¾-inch (2-cm) hem. Pin the cuff in place around the top of the stocking and stitch the cuff to the stocking by hand from the inside.

Winter White
Stocking

I have a weakness for beautiful winter white wool. Subtle textural differences among the buttons, beads, and ribbon on the cuff of this stocking provide visual interest. Mother-of-pearl, bone, glass, frosted glass, freshwater pearls, and ceramic are twisted together with gold wire and sheer ribbons. This stocking would be nice in any monochromatic scheme—perhaps in shades of purple, green, or bright red.

YOU WILL NEED

Pattern #1 (see page 116)

¼ yard (.2 m) white wool

1¼ yards (1.1 m) or more 1-inch (2.5-cm) organza ribbon, in ivory and green

Assorted buttons and beads

24-gauge gold wire, about 35 inches (91.5 cm)

INSTRUCTIONS

Construct the stocking by cutting the pieces out and stitching them together with right sides together as described on page 12 (method #1). Hem the top edge with a ¾-inch (2-cm) hem. Cut a piece for the cuff to 5½ x 17 inches (14 x 43 cm) and stitch the short edges together. Turn up ½ inch (1.5 cm) on the top and bottom edges of the cuff and hem by hand.

Place the cuff on the stocking; it will be larger than the stocking. Scrunch the fabric and pin scrunched areas in place. Continue this process until the scrunching is distributed somewhat evenly over the surface of the cuff. Stitch the cuff to the stocking, adding beads and buttons randomly as you go. Pull the thread rather tightly when stitching beads so that they are nestled into the fabric, causing additional ripples in the fabric.

Cut a piece of wire 36 inches (91.5 cm) long. With a pair of pliers, gently bend the end into a small spiral, and put a few beads on the wire. Bend the wire, or loop it around, then add another bead or two until you have gone the whole length of the wire and the entire piece is only about half as long as it began. Bend the wire around to fit on the cuff of the stocking and stitch it in place. The wire is very pliable and is easy to sew to the fabric.

To finish, weave the ribbons through the wire and around the beads and buttons and tack in place at random spots. Anchor all the elements together with a button and allow the ends of the ribbons to fall down the side of the stocking. Make a loop out of wool for a hanger, if desired, and stitch it to the inside of the stocking.

Jester Stocking

Synthetic fleece, bells, and beads in brilliant colors are combined in this playful stocking. I can't think of a color combination that wouldn't work here—the brighter the better. It's a great way to present a whimsical gift, and would also be handsome made of red and white synthetic fleece and filled with candy canes.

YOU WILL NEED

Pattern #14 (page 126)

Patterns for cuff pieces (at right)

½ yard (.5 m) purple synthetic fleece

Scraps of blue synthetic fleece for the cuff

4 bells

8 beads

INSTRUCTIONS

Stitch the stocking with wrong sides together and trim the seam allowance close to the stitching as described on page 13 (method #2).

Using the cuff pattern, cut out two blue synthetic fleece cuff pieces. Fold one blue piece in the middle and position on the front of the stocking so that the edges will be visible when the top of the purple stocking is folded down (see photograph). Pin the piece in place and stitch to the stocking. Repeat this procedure with the second blue piece on the back of the stocking.

Stitch a bell to the four front points on the purple synthetic fleece and a bead to each of the smaller, blue points underneath.

Enlarge 200%

Coffee
Stocking

My sister has a collection of star charms, and she loves to do cross-stitch—so I asked her to combine the two elements in a stocking. The embroidery in this one has a much looser feel than a cross-stitch sampler; it's worked on a large scale and doesn't take long to complete. The texture and color of the linen reminds me of the bags that coffee comes in, so it occurred to me to fill it with gourmet beans and a mug for a coffee-loving friend.

YOU WILL NEED

Pattern #1 (see page 116)

8-count brown cross-stitch fabric (linen),
12 x 16 inches (30.5 x 40.5 cm)

Felt (for backing), black or navy blue,
12 x 16 inches (30.5 x 40.5 cm)

Cotton embroidery floss, black or navy blue

Gold embroidery floss or thread

½ yard (.5 m) ⅛-inch (.3-cm) black ribbon

Star charms, about 8

Chalk

INSTRUCTIONS

Using the pattern provided, trace the stocking pattern onto the cross-stitch fabric, then draw three stars on the stocking with chalk. Use these marks as a guide to cross-stitch the stars (see page 15). Don't try for flawless stars, but rather allow them to have an imperfect appearance.

Stitch the stars with three strands of dark blue or black floss entwined with one or two strands of gold floss. When the stitching is complete, cut out the stocking shape. Next, cut the backing from the felt and sew the backing and the cross-stitch fabric together as described on page 12 (method #1). Tie charms to black ribbon and gold thread, arrange them in staggered lengths, and stitch the ends directly to the stocking.

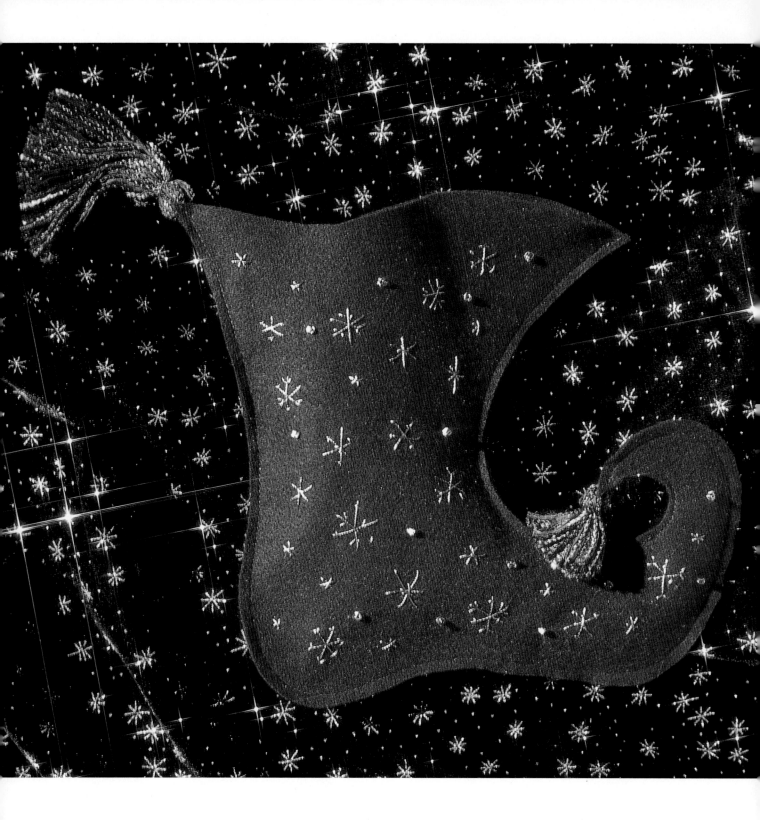

Elf Boot
Stocking

Since elves are an important part of the magic of Christmas, I decided the book would not be complete without a stocking made in the shape of an elf boot. The embroidered snowflakes and beads add to the stocking's charm. A quick variation is to make the stocking without the embroidery or beads, just a simple boot shape with tassels. A grouping of these stockings in a variety of bright colors looks great mixed with throw pillows on a contemporary couch or bed.

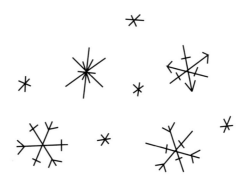

YOU WILL NEED

Pattern #6 (see page 119)

½ yard (.5 m) wool felt

Cotton or silk embroidery floss

Glass beads, about 15

2 tassels (see page 14)

INSTRUCTIONS

First, cut two stocking pieces from the felt according to the pattern. You can embroider snowflakes either on the front piece or on both the back and front pieces, depending on your preference. Use straight stitches to embroider snowflakes (see page 15). Sew on beads randomly to add shine. Be careful to stay about 1 inch (2.5 cm) away from the edge so that when you sew the front and back pieces together, you're not stitching over beads or embroidery.

Stitch the front to the back with wrong sides together as described on page 13 (method #2), either on a machine or by hand. Trim the seam allowance so that it's even and looks neat, since it is on the outside of the stocking.

Make two tassels as described on page 14. I used a variegated yarn with blues, greens, yellows, and purples. The tassel for the toe should measure approximately 1½ inch (4 cm); the one at the top of the stocking is about 3 inches (7.5 cm) in length. Stitch the tassels to the stocking.

Felt Heart
Stocking

love to make felt, partly because I'm never certain what it will look like until the end. I find this uncertainty very exciting! The heart on this stocking is handmade felt; the body was made from an old wool blanket (a flea-market find) that I felted by machine-washing it in hot water.

For the felt heart:

Cotton muslin

Wool roving in a variety of colors

Rubber bands

Needle and thread

Washing machine or a sink with very hot water and rubber gloves

For the stocking:

Pattern #4 (see page 117)

Handmade felt heart

½ yard (.5 m) wool felt, felted blanket, or white wool

Embroidery floss

Gold metallic thread

Several beads (optional)

If you apply heat and pressure to wet wool fibers, they will interlock and form felt. A wool blanket or sweater will felt simply by washing it in hot water. This is what you should do to make felt for the body of the stocking. (You can felt smaller pieces in the washer, too.) This is a fun project for kids; my sister is an art teacher, and felting is one of her students' favorite projects. Either put the piece in the dryer or air dry.

Next, make the felt heart. Wool fiber can be purchased at yarn or weaving stores in a form called *roving* (it's similar to large, loose yarn). It comes in a beautiful array of brilliant colors. For this heart, I used red, purple, and a small amount of natural white. Cut a piece of muslin about 15 inches (38 cm) square and arrange the wool fibers on it. Place the fibers so that they are distributed evenly, with the ends pointing in all different directions. Mix the red and purple roving, adding the white occasionally. Form the vague shape of a heart.

Keep piling on the fibers until the pile is several inches (5 cm) high, then put another piece of muslin over the top of the wool. With the needle and thread, baste the muslin pieces together, first in a heart shape around the outside edges of the pile of fibers, then all through the heart; this will keep the fibers in a relatively even layer so they don't all bunch up in one place. Once it's securely basted, roll the piece tightly and wrap rubber bands around it.

Put the piece in the washer in hot water (and any other wash you may be doing in hot water). When the cycle is finished, you will have felt. Remove it

Charm
Stocking

This pretty little stocking is a fun way to present a gift of jewelry. It takes very little time to construct and is easy to personalize. It's made of boiled wool, which has a beautifully textured surface; it is so tightly felted that it doesn't ravel. Boiled wool can be purchased at some better fabric stores, but this wool came from a jacket that I found in a secondhand clothing store.

YOU WILL NEED

Pattern #3 (see page 116)

¼ yard (.2 m) red boiled wool

Embroidery floss, cotton or silk

½ yard (.5 m) ribbon

Assorted beads and charms

INSTRUCTIONS

Cut the stocking pieces out according to the pattern and construct the stocking as described on page 13 (method #2). I've used two strands of cotton embroidery floss (it can be thicker if you like) in a contrasting color to stitch around the outer edge of the stocking and the top opening. Cut a strip of wool for a hanger, 1 x 7 inches (2.5 x 18 cm), stitch on both sides of the strip to form a loop, then sew it to the inside of the stocking.

The charms and beads that decorate the stocking are a wonderful opportunity to add a personalized touch. Tie the charms to a gold thread or a piece of colored embroidery floss and thread on beads. If you wish, tie knots in the thread to create space between beads. Tie a bow with the ribbon and stitch it in place where the beads are anchored.

from the washer, clip the stitches to remove the basting, and peel the layers of muslin apart to reveal the piece of felt. Once it dries, you can appliqué and embroider it. It will be roughly in the shape of a heart. Trim the piece until you are pleased with the shape. You may want to make two or three felt pieces and choose your favorite one for the stocking.

Cut the stocking pieces out according to the pattern. When the felt heart is completely dry, pin it to the front piece of the stocking and stitch it in place with two colors of twirling lines of stitches (lines of straight stitches in a swirling pattern). Sew additional swirling stitches with gold thread. Add several French knots (see page 15) and cross-stitches (see page 15).

Construct the stocking by stitching the right sides together as described on page 12 (method #1). Add a loop made from a scrap of wool, if desired.

Fringed Stocking

T his stocking is an example of how a stocking's contents can dictate
its appearance. I had the idea for it when I noticed that fuchsia
satin ribbon looked fabulous with these glass paperweights.
The fringe of glass beads was the finishing touch.

YOU WILL NEED

Pattern #1 (see page 116)

½ yard (.5 m) white wool

½ yard (.5 m) 2-inch (5-cm) satin, wire-edged
ribbon, fuchsia

½ yard (.5 cm) beaded fringe (available at
specialty fabric stores or you can make your
own [see right])

INSTRUCTIONS

Cut the stocking pieces according to the pattern
and construct the stocking as described on page 12
(method #1) without finishing the top edge.

Baste the beaded fringe to the edge of the satin ribbon
so that only the fringe is visible (not the twill tape).
Stitch the ends of the ribbon together (forming a cuff),
then pin the ribbon to the top of the stocking. Create
interest by using the wire in the ribbon to shape the
ribbon in a wavy pattern. Pin ribbon in place.

Carefully stitch the ribbon to the stocking along the
beaded edge. Stitch on the edge of the ribbon, so that
the basting stitches can be removed. It's hard to hide
your stitches on the satin ribbon, so make certain your
thread matches as closely as possible and keep your
stitches very small.

MAKING BEADED FRINGE

YOU WILL NEED

Twill tape

Beading needle

Assortment of beads

Thread to match the beads

INSTRUCTIONS

Beaded fringe is beautiful and not difficult to
make; it just takes time and planning. First, you
have to determine how long and how far apart
each fringe will be. The fringe I have used is 1½
inches (4 cm) long and ½ inch (1.5 cm) apart.

Begin by threading your needle and knotting the
end. Bring the needle through the twill tape very
close to the edge. Then bring the needle through
the beads you have chosen for the fringe. Once you
get to the last bead, bring the needle back through
all of the beads so that you come out back at the
twill tape where you started. Tie off the thread and
repeat the process again ½ inch (1.5 cm) from the
first fringe.

Georgene's Favorite
Stocking

This contemporary velvet stocking features lovely contrasts in textures and colors. Making it out of white velvet (with gold accents) and filling it with gifts wrapped in white paper and tied with gold ribbon also makes for a stunning presentation.

YOU WILL NEED

Pattern #4 (see page 117)

¼ yard (.2 m) velvet for the stocking

¼ yard (.2 m) velvet for the cuff

½ yard (.5 m) 4-inch (10-cm) gold metallic ribbon with wired edges

½ yard (5 m) ⅛-inch (.3-cm) ribbon, red, green, and purple

1 package tiny gold beads

1 piece thin craft foam, 5 inches (12.5 cm) square

Gold acrylic paint

15 inches (38 cm) gold wire

Assorted glass and metallic beads

INSTRUCTIONS

Begin by cutting a star from the foam with a sharp knife. Paint the star shape with the gold paint. You may have to use two or three coats to get a good finish. Cut two stocking pieces from green velvet and sew the pieces with right sides together as described on page 12 (method #1). Finish the top edge with a ¾-inch (2-cm) hem.

Cut a piece, 20 x 17 inches (51 x 43 cm), from the purple velvet to make the cuff. Stitch the long edges together to form a tube, then stitch the ends together to form a doughnut-shaped piece. (The cuff will be larger than the top of the stocking to allow for scrunching the fabric.)

Scrunch the velvet in the cuff, pin the scrunched fabric in place on the stocking, then adjust the cuff until the appearance is balanced and appealing. With matching thread, stitch the folds in place, sewing through all layers so that the cuff is joined to the stocking at the same time. Next, use matching thread and a beading needle to stitch around the upper and lower edges of the cuff. Add beads randomly to the top of the cuff. Pull the thread very tightly, so that the fabric bunches up somewhat and the beads become tucked into the fabric.

Wrap the wide ribbon around the cuff, then wrap the three narrow ribbons over top of the wide ribbon. Arrange the narrow ribbons and tack them in place by randomly stitching beads on top of them. Stitch all the ribbons together on the back or, if you have enough ribbon, simply tie them in a knot or bow on the back side.

To finish, cut a piece of gold wire about 15 inches (38 cm) long and thread beads onto it. You can even add letters to spell a name or someone's initials. In between the beads, twist and turn the wire to create interesting shapes; position the wire on the cuff of the stocking so that it wraps around the gold star. Stitch the wire to the stocking; the wire will hold the star in place.

Gypsy
Stocking

This colorful stocking is my favorite, partly because I had so much fun creating it. It takes very little time to put together, but creates the opposite impression—possibly due to its many layers of colors and beads. I've provided patterns for my shapes, but you can use any shapes that appeal to you. The letters of someone's name (in any order) makes for a personalized stocking with pizzazz.

YOU WILL NEED

Pattern #13 (see page 125)

Patterns for felt cutouts (at right)

½ yard (.5 m) black wool felt

Wool felt scraps for appliqués in contrasting colors

Cotton embroidery floss in assorted colors

Red glass beads, about 50

6 ribbons, varying in color, width, and length
(from ½ yard [.5 m] to 1½ yards [1.3 m])

INSTRUCTIONS

Using the pattern, cut two stocking shapes from the black felt. Determine which side of the stocking will be the front. For this stocking, the two pieces will be sewn together last.

Trace the patterns for the cutouts onto the felt. Cut the shapes from the felt and pin them to the front of the stocking as shown in the photograph. In some cases, you will need to layer the pieces. Stitch the felt pieces down with large, bold stitches as shown. The stitches will serve as a decoration as well as to secure the appliqués in place. Stitch on the beads in the same way, using them to accent and outline the felt shapes.

Stitch the front piece to the back piece with wrong sides together, either using a sewing machine or by hand as described on page 13 (method #2). Gather the ribbons together and tie a knot in the center of all of them. Stitch the knot to the inside of the stocking; a loop for a hanger can be made with one of these ribbons.

Enlarge 200%

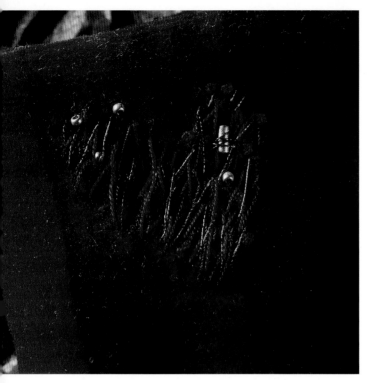

Heart
Stocking

I consider myself blessed to have a friend who is a fiber artist. Carolyn Kallenborn makes gorgeous garments from her textile creations—and her scraps have been the inspiration for a number of my stockings. The red velvet on the cuff of this stocking is one of her pieces. The shape of a heart was suggested in the pattern, so I chose to emphasize it with stitching and beads. The result is an exciting, contemporary stocking. A simple heart embroidered on a solid-red velvet cuff also works well.

YOU WILL NEED

Pattern #1 (see page 116)

¼ yard (.2 m) black velvet

Red velvet, printed or solid (for cuff), 11 x 16 inches (28 x 40.5 cm)

Cotton embroidery thread, red and black

Red metallic thread

Several gold beads

INSTRUCTIONS

Carolyn's fabric is a cotton velvet that has been printed with a direct application of thickened fiber-reactive dyes in varying shades to create a gradation of color. She applies the dye with sheets of clear acrylic. The background is colored with shades of red, and the black is applied with smaller rectangles of clear acrylic sheeting. The dye is simply painted on the sheeting, then the sheeting is stamped onto the fabric.

Begin by embroidering the heart. Use long stitches to fill in the area of the heart, intermixing the different threads. Tie French knots (see page 15) randomly throughout the heart, and add some beads as you work. Next, make the red velvet piece into a cuff. Stitch the long edges together, then the short edges together to form a doughnut-shaped piece of fabric.

Make the body of the stocking from the black velvet: Cut two pieces according to the pattern and stitch right sides together as described on page 12 (method #1). Turn the stocking right side out. Finish the top edge with a ¾-inch (2-cm) hem. Pin the cuff in place and stitch to the stocking by hand.

Kimono Stocking

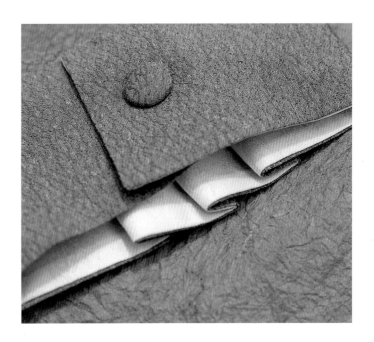

Subtle color variations in the silk give this stocking a lovely, almost iridescent appearance. I found the fabric on a Japanese kimono at a consignment shop. Kimonos are a great source of inspiration for me, not only because of the unusual fabrics and beautiful construction, but because of the unexpected details often found inside; in fact, the lining fabric is sometimes more interesting than the outside of the garment. Also, kimonos often have interesting braids or ribbon ties as closures. This one had covered buttons, which are not usually associated with kimonos; I made use of these on the cuff.

YOU WILL NEED

Pattern #1 (see page 116)

¼ yard (.2 m) silk, preferably from an old kimono

Lining fabric for the cuff (possibly from another part of the kimono)

4 covered ¾-inch (2-cm) buttons

INSTRUCTIONS

Construct the stocking: Cut two silk pieces according to the pattern and sew the pieces with the right sides together as described on page 12 (method #1). Turn the stocking with right sides out. Finish the top edge with a ¾-inch (2-cm) hem.

Cut a piece of silk fabric and a piece of lining fabric for the cuff; each piece should measure 4 x 18½ inches (10 x 47 cm). Stitch the cuff fabric to the lining, with right sides together on three sides. Trim the seam allowances, turn, and press. Stitch the open end closed to create a long band for the cuff.

Press three ½-inch (1.5-cm) pleats in the center of the band and baste them in place. Position the cuff over the top edge of the stocking and pin in place. Wrap the ends of the band around the back of the stocking and overlap the ends. Stitch the cuff to the stocking from the inside. To finish, sew on the covered buttons, three on the front (one centered on each pleat) and one on the back where the ends overlap (see detail photograph).

Winter Moon
Stocking

This tall, skinny stocking is an ideal container for gifts that are reminiscent of the great outdoors. It was inspired by memories of moonlit walks in the pine forest of northern Wisconsin.

YOU WILL NEED

Pattern #10 (see page 123)

Patterns for moonlit design (below)

¼ yard (.2 m) blue wool, 54 inches wide (137 cm)

Scraps of white, brown, and green wool

Green embroidery floss

Pearl beads, approximately 150

Metallic green thread

INSTRUCTIONS

First, cut all the pieces out according to the patterns: two blue stocking pieces, one white snow, one white moon, 30 green tree branches, and two brown tree trunks. If you use high-quality wool, you will not need to turn the edges under before you stitch the pieces in place; I have not here. Begin by stitching the white wool "snow" over the foot of the front stocking piece, using small stitches. Then stitch the moon and the tree trunks to the stocking.

Pin the tree branch pieces to the stocking, layering as you go to imitate branches. Stitch them in place with long stitches of green metallic embroidery floss. Sew on beads to imitate falling snow as well as a snow pile at the top of the hill. Finally, stitch the stocking front to the back as described on page 12 (method #1) and finish the top edge with a ¾-inch (2-cm) hem. Make a blue wool loop (see page 13) and stitch to the inside of the stocking.

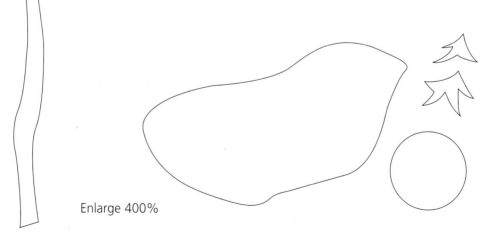

Enlarge 400%

Quilted Angel
Stocking

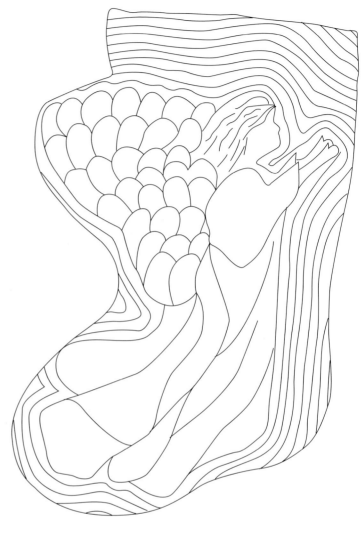

Enlarge 400%

Angels are a favorite subject matter for expert quilter Joyce Abernathy, who quilted this stocking. I altered the traditional stocking shape to accommodate the wing of the angel, and the overall height of the finished stocking is 21 inches (53.5 cm). An alternative is to make the angel smaller and have more quilted lines around it.

YOU WILL NEED

Pattern #9 (page 122)

Angel pattern (at right)

½ yard (.5 m) blue fabric for the body

Muslin for backing, 18 x 24 inches (45.5 x 61 cm)

Thin batting, 18 x 24 inches (45.5 x 61 cm)

Metallic gold thread

1½ yards (1.4 m) 4-inch (10-cm) gold ribbon

Fabric pen or chalk

INSTRUCTIONS

Use the pattern provided to trace the design on the stocking with a fabric pen. Joyce transfers the image to her fabric before she quilts it by taping it to a window and tracing it. (She says her sliding glass door is often completely covered with fabric.) This is an effective method for transferring the angel design onto the fabric for this stocking.

Cut out the stocking pieces, batting, and backing according to the pattern, and fasten the layers together with safety pins. With a very close zigzag stitch on your sewing machine, or with a straight quilting stitch by hand, follow the image you have traced onto the fabric. When you've finished the angel, quilt around the design in rows approximately ¼ inch (.5 cm) apart. This is called *echo quilting*.

Sew the front piece to the back piece of the stocking as described on page 12 (method #1) and finish the top edge with a ¾-inch (2-cm) hem. Tie a large bow with the gold ribbon and stitch to the stocking.

Rhinestone Stocking

Black velvet, hand-dyed silk, and rhinestone buttons are combined in a stunning stocking worthy of even the most elegant holiday celebration. Wrap a bottle of champagne and pretty champagne glasses in gold tissue, tuck inside the stocking, and give to the friend who celebrates New Year's with wild abandon.

YOU WILL NEED

Pattern #5 (see page 118)

½ yard (.5 m) black velvet

2½ yards (2.3 m) 2½-inch (6.5-cm) hand-dyed silk ribbon

½ yard (.5 m) black grosgrain ribbon

Assortment of rhinestone buttons (approximately 16) in varying sizes and shapes

½ yard (.5 m) lining fabric or 1 yard (.9 m) ribbon for facing

INSTRUCTIONS

Use the pattern to construct the stocking from black velvet as described on page 12 (method #1). Either line the stocking (see page 13) or finish the top edge with a yard (.9 m) of 1½-inch (4-cm) ribbon as facing. Pin the edge of the ribbon to the top edge of the stocking with right sides together. Stitch with a ¼-inch (.5-cm) seam allowance. Fold the ribbon to the inside of the stocking and press. Tack loose edge of ribbon in place.

Stitch the rhinestones to the center of the grosgrain ribbon (as shown in the detail photograph) until you have covered about 8 inches (20.5 cm) of the ribbon with buttons. Stitch the grosgrain ribbon to the silk ribbon and position around the top of the stocking. Stitch in place.

Fast and Fun Stockings

Fifties Tablecloth
Stocking

Flea markets and garage sales are wonderful sources of interesting printed linens from the 40s and 50s. It is not unusual to find tablecloths in perfect condition, though sometimes only parts of them are useable. This stocking is charming hanging in a kitchen window during the Christmas season; it's also a fun and unusual way to deliver holiday cookies to a friend.

YOU WILL NEED

Pattern #4 (see page 117)

Antique tablecloth fabric, 18 x 24 inches (45.5 x 51 cm)

Ribbon or rickrack (optional)

INSTRUCTIONS

The stocking is cut using pattern #4 on page 117, but if you can find only a small piece of tablecloth in good condition, use a smaller pattern and make a smaller stocking. Before you cut, determine the portion of the pattern that you wish to appear on the stocking. Cut the pieces out and sew the front to the back with right sides together as described on page 12 (method #1). Finish the top edge by pressing in 1 inch (2.5 cm) and hemming. You can make a loop out of the same fabric (see page 13) or sew a piece of ribbon or rickrack to the inside of the stocking for a hanger.

Kitchen Towel
Stocking

bright kitchen towel makes a fun gift stocking for a person who loves to cook, especially when filled with a cookbook, gourmet delicacies, and fancy kitchen utensils.

YOU WILL NEED

Pattern #4 (see page 117)

New kitchen towel (possibly two towels, if you want to match the pattern front and back)

INSTRUCTIONS

Using pattern #4 on page 117, cut out the stocking pieces. If you are using two towels, spend some time arranging the pattern so that the design will match, front and back. Sew the pieces with right sides together as described on page 12 (method #1). Trim and clip seams and turn right side out. Finish top edge of the stocking by pressing down 1 inch (2.5 cm) at the top and hemming. Fill with something delicious and deliver!

THEME STOCKINGS

Filling a stocking for someone who has a special hobby or interest is fun, and having a theme in mind sometimes makes the task easier. For a coffee lover, fill a stocking (possibly one made from a burlap coffee bag) with a pound of gourmet coffee, something delicious to eat (a muffin, scone, or coffee cake, perhaps), and a pretty handmade ceramic mug. Another fun idea is to make a stocking from fabric in someone's favorite color, and fill the stocking with items in that color. Imagine a solid green stocking embellished with green embroidery and green ribbon, and filled with green toys, books, and trinkets. For an art student, make the stocking out of canvas (ready to be painted, either by you or the recipient), and fill it with art supplies. The possibilities for theme stockings are endless, so use your imagination.

Plaid Silk Shantung
Stocking

Some fabrics are so gorgeous they require very little embellishment. This plaid silk shantung has a wonderful textured surface and seems almost to glow in the light. A long, narrow shape makes good use of ¼ yard (.2 m) of silk—with as little waste as possible. I chose a favorite button from my collection to stitch on the ribbon and to give the stocking some added interest. Using buttons from meaningful garments as accents in Christmas stockings is a great way to enjoy these cherished buttons for years to come. Three or four of these stockings hung together on a mantel are a stunning holiday decoration.

YOU WILL NEED

Pattern #7 (see page 120)

¼ yard (.2 m) plaid silk shantung

2 yards (1.8 cm) 2-inch (5-cm) satin ribbon

Decorative button

INSTRUCTIONS

For this project, the challenge is finding the right piece of fabric; once you have a beautiful piece of silk, the construction of the stocking is very simple. Using the pattern, cut the pieces from the fabric so that the top edge of the stocking is on the selvage.

I did finish the top edge of this stocking, because the selvage had character—and it will not ravel. This also allowed me to make the stocking about an inch (2.5 cm) longer. Stitch the stocking pieces together as described on page 12 (method #1). If you decide to finish off the top edge, do so next by pressing 1 inch (2.5 cm) to the inside and stitching in place. Tie a knot and bow in the center of the satin ribbon and stitch the bow to the stocking. Sew the button on top of the bow and voila!

Miniature Felt
Stocking

My sister designed this precious little stocking by cutting the shapes out of paper. It is really more of an ornament or decoration than a practical stocking—it's approximately 5 inches (12.5 cm) tall and very lightweight.

YOU WILL NEED

Pattern #12 (see page 125)

Wool felt, red and green, each piece about 6 inches (15 cm) square

½ yard (.5 cm) each red and green ⅛-inch (.3-cm) ribbon

INSTRUCTIONS

Trace the heart pattern onto paper and cut it out. A pair of very small scissors will make cutting the heart shapes much easier. Pin the pattern to the red felt and cut around the outside edges to create the back piece. Don't cut the hearts from this piece. Then pin the pattern securely to the green felt and cut around it. Use small, sharp scissors to carefully cut out the design. Another option is to trace the pattern onto the felt with a fabric pen or chalk, remove the pattern, then cut the pattern out.

Place the green piece over the red piece and use matching green thread to stitch the edges together by hand with tiny stitches. To finish, hold the two ribbons together, fold them in half, and tie a knot (joining the ribbons). Stitch the knot to the edge of the stocking for a hanger.

HOME DECORATING WITH STOCKINGS

Don't wait until Christmas Eve to bring out your stockings. And don't confine your handmade treasures to the mantle, either. Stuff crumpled tissue paper in stockings (to add body without adding weight) and hang them wherever they can be admired and look festive. Add a few items to the top to make the stocking look full—a candy cane or an ornament serves this purpose well. There are many places in your house where you can hang stockings as decorations. Try doorknobs, window latches, dresser knobs, and drawer pulls. Hanging a stocking on the front door is a festive way to greet guests. Or what about the mailbox? Tie stockings to the backs of chairs, to headboards, on mirrors, or to the edge of a shelf. Indeed, you'll be surprised at how gorgeous stockings are all over your house!

Potato-Printed
Stocking

Although these are perfect stockings for kids to make, adults can enjoy the process as well. The finished stockings, lined with colored cellophane, are a fun way to present holiday cookies to a classmate or a child's favorite teacher at the school Christmas party.

YOU WILL NEED

Pattern #4 (see page 117)

Paper grocery bags (or brown craft paper)

Potatoes

Sharp paring knife

Acrylic paints in assorted colors

Paintbrush

Rubber cement

INSTRUCTIONS

Begin by tracing the stocking pattern on brown paper bags or craft paper; cut out the stocking shapes. To make the potato stamps, first thoroughly wash the potatoes and cut each potato in half to create a smooth surface. Cut any shape into the surface with a knife. You can draw on the surface of the potato with a marker first if it helps, but perfection doesn't count in this project—the best prints are from irregular shapes. Before you begin potato printing, press the surface of the potato design on paper towels to dry, so you'll have clearer images when you begin to print. Use a paintbrush to apply the paint to the potato design, then stamp the shapes onto the stocking.

Once the paint is dry, attach the front stocking piece to the back piece, using rubber cement: Brush on a ½-inch-wide (1.5-cm) strip of cement on the outer edges of the back side of the stocking pieces. Press the two pieces together. When the glue is dry, trim the edges so they are even.

Purple Star
Stocking

Use soft synthetic fleece to make fun and colorful stockings for kids. It is extremely easy to sew and, like felt, the edges of synthetic fleece will not ravel. The size of this stocking allows tiny hands to reach all the way to the bottom—fill with goodies and give as a favor at a children's party.

YOU WILL NEED

Pattern #2 (see page 116)

¼ yard (.2 m) purple synthetic fleece

Small wooden stars with center holes (available at craft stores)

Acrylic paint (red, blue, and purple)

Paintbrush

½ yard (.5 m) ⅛-inch (.3-cm) ribbon, red and blue

Gold crinkle wire or fine wire and pliers

3 small gold beads

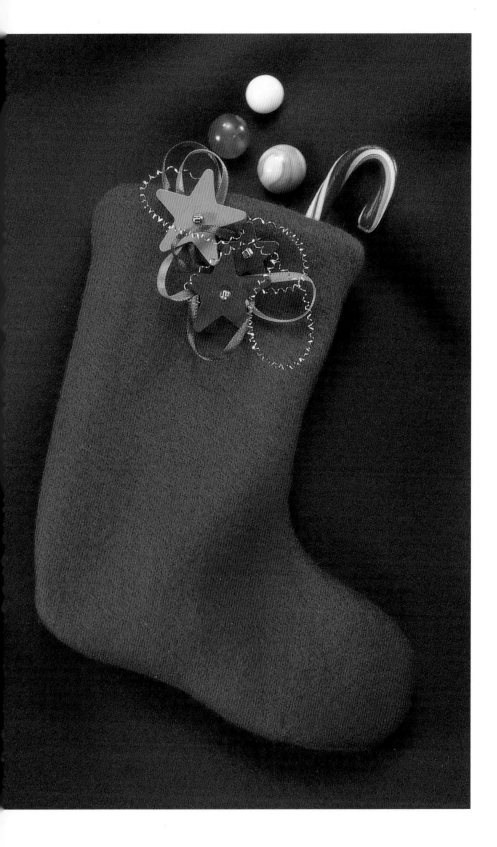

Begin by using the pattern to cut the stocking pieces out of synthetic fleece. Sew the pieces with right sides together as described on page 12 (method #1). Fold in ¾ inch (2 cm) on the top edge and hem.

To decorate the stocking, paint the wooden stars different colors (blue, red, and purple). When the stars are dry, arrange them on the upper edge of the stocking, overlapping them slightly. To attach the stars, bring a needle and thread up through the fabric, the star, then the bead—then back down through the star and fabric. Tie thread on back side of fabric to anchor the stars in place. *Note:* sometimes wooden stars are available without holes; in this case, you will need to drill holes with an electric drill.

Cut an 8-inch (20.5-cm) length of red ribbon and tack one edge of the ribbon to the stocking beneath one of the stars. Twist and loop the ribbon around and continue to tack it under the edges of the stars so that the stitches are not visible. It takes only three or four loops to fill up the space and add color to the stars. Repeat this process with the blue ribbon and the gold crinkle wire. If you want to make a larger stocking in this manner, simply add more stars to the cluster and use more ribbon colors.

Simple Felt
Stocking

If you want to make stockings for all your favorite kids for Christmas—and you don't have much time—this is the stocking I would suggest. It's a fun, bright stocking that is extremely easy to make. The back of this stocking has an extension tab that ties on the front to form a hanger.

YOU WILL NEED

Pattern #15 (see page 127)

½ yard (.5 m) white wool felt

¼ yard (.2 m) purple wool felt

1½ yard (1.4 m) ⅛-inch (.3-cm) ribbon in two colors

Rotary cutter, cutting surface, and a "wave" blade (or pinking blade); pinking shears; or scallop shears

INSTRUCTIONS

Trace the two stocking patterns onto the felt (purple front piece and white back piece), then cut the pieces out carefully with a rotary cutter and a wave blade. Rotary cutters are very common and found in fabric stores or crafts-supply stores. You can also use pinking shears or scallop shears for this purpose.

Once the pieces are cut, pin the purple felt onto the white felt, and stitch in place, either with a sewing machine or by hand. Fold the extension (on the white piece) from the back onto the purple felt piece in the front. Cut two slits in the end of the white extension and matching slits in the purple piece. Slide the ribbon through these slits and tie into a bow.

THE PERSONAL TOUCH

Personalizing stockings is great fun. If you are using stockings as gift wrapping and don't want to put names on the stockings themselves, consider making labels. Cut interesting shapes out of beautiful paper—handmade paper works well—and use colored or metallic markers or a calligraphy pen to write the name of the recipient on the tag. Attach the tags to the stocking with pretty ribbon. If you're not confident about your handwriting, use rubber stamps for the lettering. You can stamp on paper or directly on a ribbon (test it first).

Transparent
Stocking

Who could resist filling this unusual stocking with wonderfully scented soaps and hanging it from the bathroom door on Christmas morning? Consider carefully what will go inside, since, with this one, nothing is hidden.

YOU WILL NEED

Pattern #4 (page 117)

½ yard (.5 m) very sheer gold lamé

2 yards (1.8 m) transparent ribbon

1 transparent plastic button

INSTRUCTIONS

Cut the stocking pieces out according to pattern #4 and sew the pieces with right sides together as described on page 12 (method #1). Gather the center part of the ribbon and secure it to the stocking by stitching a transparent button over top of it.

I chose not to finish the inside seam allowances of this stocking, because you can see through the fabric, and I did not want a heavy, dark edge to be visible; instead, I trimmed the seam allowances evenly and left them, knowing they would ravel and that the stocking would be somewhat fragile. That being said, feel free to finish the seam allowances for a more durable stocking.

Nontraditional Stockings

Wooden Stocking

M y father, a woodworker, volunteered to make this stocking. It's the perfect size to hang in a window (from a pretty ribbon), and the hollow center has plenty of room for goodies, anything from woodworking tools to dried flowers and evergreens.

YOU WILL NEED

Pattern #2 (see page 116)

3 standard clear pine boards,
1 x 6 x 7 inches (2.5 x 15 x 18 cm)

Wood glue

Clamps

Coping saw, scroll saw, or band saw
(for cutting out the shapes)

Gouge, chisel, and mallet, or a 2-inch
(5-cm) drum sander in an electric drill
(for forming the cavity)

Wood rasp, spokeshave, disc sander, or belt
sander clamped in vise (for shaping)

Sandpaper

Clear polyurethane

Paintbrush

INSTRUCTIONS

Pine was chosen for the stocking, because it's widely available, soft and thus easily worked with hand tools. (Note that the actual dimensions of a standard 1 x 6 is really ¾ x 5½ inches.) For this stocking, you will need a front pieces, a center piece, and a back piece. First, examine the three pieces of wood to determine which you would like for the front, center, and back of the stocking; the center piece, since it will be the least visible, should be made from the least attractive piece of wood. Trace the pattern onto the pieces of wood. Cut out the stocking shapes with a saw.

Next, remove the wood from the piece that will form the central portion of the cavity. Use a gouge, chisel, and mallet or a 2-inch (5-cm) drum sander in an electric drill. The center stocking shape will eventually have a U-shaped hole. Then enlarge the hollowed-out area by removing additional material from the adjoining front and back pieces. This can be done either with a gouge and chisel or with a 2-inch (5-cm) disk sander mounted on a drill. No more than ⅜-inch (1-cm) depth should be removed from these areas in order to achieve a nice shape.

Once the rough shape has been cut and the spaces for the cavity created, glue the pieces together and clamp. Leave them to stand overnight; follow glue manufacturer's instructions.

When the stocking is dry, remove from the clamps and begin shaping the exterior. Be careful not to remove too

Chicken Wire
Stocking

This project is a great opportunity to dig into your button box and pull out all of your green and red buttons. Green chicken wire, which I happened upon by chance in the hardware store, was the inspiration for this stocking. Put it on your front door to let visitors know you have a wonderful (albeit nontraditional) sense of holiday spirit.

much wood, or the cavity will be exposed. If you are using a rasp or a spokeshave, the work should be clamped into a vise and the material removed from the sides to the edge. Carefully round the sides towards the edge of the center piece. If you're using a belt sander, make certain that the sander is clamped securely in place. Then, holding the stocking in hand, carefully shape.

When the desired shape is complete, drill a hole for the hanger. Sand the stocking by hand and finish it however you wish. This stocking has been finished with a coat of polyurethane. You can also use stain for a darker finish or paint the stocking. Attach a ribbon or string for a hanger, if desired.

YOU WILL NEED

Pattern #1 (see page 116)

Green chicken wire, about 12 x 20 inches
(30.5 x 51 cm)

Copper wire with plastic coating
in assorted colors

Assorted buttons in red and green

White wire (for the star shapes), 8 to
10 inches (20.5 x 25.5 cm) for each star

Rickrack

Wire cutters

INSTRUCTIONS

Pin the stocking pattern to the chicken wire just as you would a piece of fabric. Cut out two pieces with wire cutters.

To attach the two parts of the stocking (the two pieces of chicken wire), use pliers to loop the wire edges around each other so that the pieces stay together. Use the colored wire to "sew" the buttons to the stocking. To finish, I added two wire star shapes that I bent out of white wire. A length of rickrack is an appropriate choice for a hanger.

Metal
Stocking

This project is a welcome change of pace from the traditional fabric stocking. Eric Ferguson, the talent behind the photography in this book, created the design. Rusted sheet metal has a wonderful color and texture, and, since the weather will not harm it, makes for a great outdoor stocking—try it on the front door or gate. Though this stocking is not difficult to construct, it does require strength and patience.

YOU WILL NEED

Pattern #4 (see page 117)

Piece of rusty sheet metal, 2-feet (.3-m) square

Nibbler sheet metal cutter

Sheet metal shears

Heavy chunk of steel or square block of oak or hard maple

Ballpeen hammer (preferably) or any other hammer

INSTRUCTIONS

Trace the pattern onto the piece of steel, then use a nibbler to cut out the stocking shapes approximately ½ inch (1.5 cm) larger all the way around. Once the shapes are cut (and you have several blisters for your effort), make a straight cut in to the traced pattern line with the shears every ½ inch (1.5 cm) or so around the outside curves of the toe and the heel. These cuts allow the sheet metal to form a curve.

Next, place the metal face up on the steel or hardwood surface you will use for pounding, with approximately ½ inch (1.5 cm) extending beyond the edge of the pounding surface. From the top, begin to hammer the ½-inch (1.5-cm) edge of metal to an angle not quite 90° from the surface. Work the edge to a curve.

The front ankle, an inner curve, is a bit tricky. There are two ways to deal with it. One is to bend it, a bit at a time, over the entire radius. The second way is to snip the metal at the center of the curve to relieve the stress and allow a more radical bending. The outer curves of the toe and heel, which you have cut into tabs at ½-inch (1.5-cm) intervals, are easy to shape. The tabs layer one onto another as you progress around the curves.

Repeat this process with the other metal piece (the other side). This time, don't bend the edge of the metal at quite as extreme an angle. You should have one side of the stocking that has its edges bent to 80° to 85°; the second side is bent to 75° to 80°. When you put the two halves together, one edge should fit inside the other. When this is achieved, pound one edge over so that it wraps together, forming an interlocking edge.

Grapevine
Stocking

All the ingredients for this stocking are natural and came from my backyard. This design works well outside as well as inside, and the variations are endless. Dried grasses can be woven in like ribbons, and herbs or dried flowers from the garden can be tucked in randomly. The only trick is to think about it early enough in the season to dry leaves, herbs, and so forth. Dried materials can be placed across the top to form a cuff, or the entire stocking can be covered for a wonderfully wild look. I've chosen soft tones for this one, though another option is to attach a few dried red roses and a long satin ribbon.

YOU WILL NEED

Pattern #4 (see page 117)

Grapevines or other flexible vine

Copper wire, about 48 inches (122 cm)

Electrical tape or other tape

Assorted naturals

Hot glue

INSTRUCTIONS

Here, I've used pattern #4 (page 117), but feel free to use any pattern; the pattern will be determined, to some degree, by how much vine is available. Begin by bending copper wire around the pattern. Don't panic about making the shape perfect, just try to get the basic stocking shape. When you've woven the wire all the way around the pattern, from top to bottom, cut the wire off and tape the ends together. This forms a framework around which you can wind the vines.

Strip the leaves from the vines and begin winding the vines around the outer edge of the wire stocking. When the outer edges are covered with vines, weave vines from one side to the other, up, down, crosswise, and in and out, until the stocking is covered with vine to your liking.

Next, add any other embellishments of your choosing. If you gather leaves when they are soft and supple, they can be stitched together with a needle and thread, then left to dry for a few days. The garland of leaves can be attached—along with all sorts of other decorations—with hot glue.

Gold Paper
Stocking

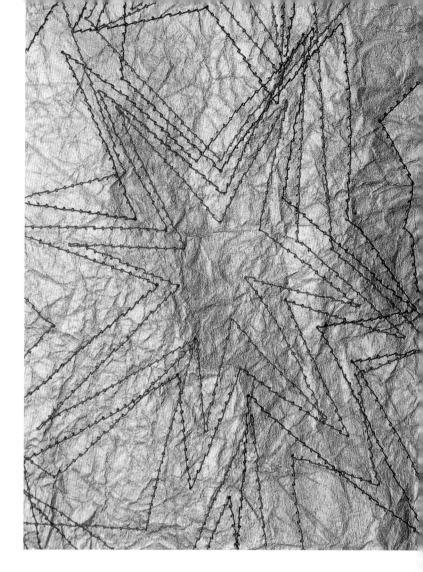

A stocking made of high-quality paper (with a high cotton content) is much stronger that you'd expect. This stocking would be beautiful without the machine stitching, or with someone's name stitched on it. It's a fun stocking to give stationery or other paper gifts in, and, though it takes time to do the stitching, it's an inexpensive gift.

YOU WILL NEED

Pattern #4 (see page 117)

One large sheet of gold paper with a crinkly finish

Sewing machine

Thread in four or five different colors

INSTRUCTIONS

Using the pattern, cut two stocking pieces out of the paper (make sure you have a front and a back). Determine which piece will be the front. Begin by drawing a star shape very lightly on the piece of paper with a pencil and stitching over the shape carefully on the sewing machine. (Keep in mind that erasing the pencil marks later isn't an option on some papers, because it can ruin the gold finish.) Continue stitching stars around the first one, echoing its shape.

Change your thread color and repeat this process. Keep stitching until you have a series of stars covering the entire stocking. After you have done this with three or four colors, or after you are satisfied with the appearance of the stocking, pin the back of the stocking to the front and stitch them together as described on page 13 (method #2). Make a paper loop out of gold paper and stitch in place to the inside of the stocking.

White Envelope
Stocking

This is a simple stocking that doesn't take long to make, but one that is easily personalized. The key to its success is using high-quality paper that can be sewn on the sewing machine. Though paper can be sewn like fabric, it won't tolerate the same amount of strain, so be careful what you put inside this stocking. Try theater tickets, a small book, stationery, or a gift box.

YOU WILL NEED

Pattern #11 (see page 124: both front and back pieces)

1 sheet of high-quality paper, preferably handmade

Sealing wax

Small scraps of thread or ribbon

Tiny bells or beads

INSTRUCTIONS

Cut out the stocking and stitch it up with wrong sides together as described on page 13 (method #2). Fold the top down and drip sealing wax where the two pieces join.

I tied tiny bells on gold thread and put the ends of the threads in the sealing wax before I stamped it. This is a good spot to personalize the stocking by using favorite colors of threads or by adding charms. Also, consider using a personalized stamp, such as an initial. Almost any narrow thread or ribbon and beads can be added to the wax for decoration. Natural accents can also be used: tiny sticks, pine cones, dried leaves, or holly leaves, for example. The wax can be stamped with a variety of items—anything that won't melt down in the hot wax. A button or piece of silverware that leaves an impression works well.

You can also make the seal on a piece of wax paper, peel it off when it dries, and attach it to the stocking with rubber cement. This prevents the seal from being destroyed when the package is opened and allows you to make several seals in different variations before choosing the best look for the stocking.

Seashell
Stocking

Because I have always lived in a northern climate, snow and evergreens characterize Christmas for me. But, of course, some people spend Christmas on the beach. My sister designed this one; she combined the texture of gesso with seashells to create a beautiful stocking for those who spend the holidays at the shore. Gesso is available at art supply stores; it's used to prime canvases before painting with oils.

YOU WILL NEED

Pattern #2 (see page 116)

Cotton muslin, 12 x 9 inches (30.5 x 23 cm)

Small seashells

Gesso

Silk embroidery floss

Natural-colored thread

Rotary cutter with wave blade or scallop shears

INSTRUCTIONS

Cut a piece of muslin to approximately 12 x 9 inches (30.5 x 23 cm) and paint it with gesso. When the gesso is dry, fold the fabric in half and cut the stocking out about ½ inch (1.5 cm) larger than the pattern, with the longest curved surface of the stocking placed on the fold. (You will cut only one piece for this stocking, but it will actually be two stocking pieces connected at the fold.)

Holding the stocking steady, cut around the edges with the rotary cutter or scallop shears. This takes quite a bit of pressure, because you are cutting though two layers. Open the stocking back out, arrange the shells, and stitch them in place. Using natural-colored thread, sew through any tiny holes in the shells or over the starfish or coral. Next, fold the stocking and stitch the front to the back by placing French knots (see page 15) around the edge of the stocking with silk embroidery floss. *Note:* you do not use either of the basic methods to construct this stocking.

Beaded Wire
Stocking

Although wire may not be a traditional material for making holiday decorations, it can be shaped easily into a festive stocking. The addition of glass beads provides color and texture; I chose beads in a variety of colors, though using only clear or frosted beads creates a more elegant stocking. You can vary the design by placing the beads only around the top edge of the stocking to create a beaded cuff. When hung from a tall crystal candlestick by a satin ribbon, this stocking makes a spectacular centerpiece for a holiday table.

YOU WILL NEED

Pattern #2 (see page 116)

Piece of cardboard

1 spool silver craft wire

Assorted glass beads, approximately 30

Small needle-nose pliers

INSTRUCTIONS

This stocking takes some patience, but it is well worth the effort. To begin, cut pattern #2 out of a piece of cardboard, then cut ½-inch (1.5-cm) slits into the cardboard around the outside edges (except for the top edge). You will use these slits to hold the wire in place as you weave around the cardboard pattern.

Cut a 3-foot (.9-m) length of wire from the spool. First, bend one end of the wire to secure it in a slit in the top of the cardboard. Begin to loop the wire around the top edge of the cardboard. With pliers or by hand, make shapes and loops in the wire and add beads randomly as you work by slipping beads onto the wire. If you have

difficulty keeping the wire in the slit, secure the wire to the cardboard with tape. Once you have shaped the wire around the top of the cardboard, begin to work down the rest of the pattern, bending and looping the wire as you go, wrapping it around the cardboard pattern and tucking it into the slits to hold it in place.

Randomly weave the wire in and out of other wires as you work to create structural stability in the stocking. When you've used up the first length of wire, twist the end around another wire and begin again with another piece of wire. Work all the way around the cardboard pattern, using the slits to keep the wire in place along the edges. (This is where patience comes in.) Keep at it, weaving until both sides of the cardboard pattern are evenly covered, and you are satisfied with the appearance.

Next, gently pull the wire from the slits in the cardboard and slide the cardboard out of the stocking. You'll find the stocking is rather malleable and can be reshaped gently if it stretched out of shape when the pattern was removed. Make a wire loop or tie a piece of ribbon to form a loop.

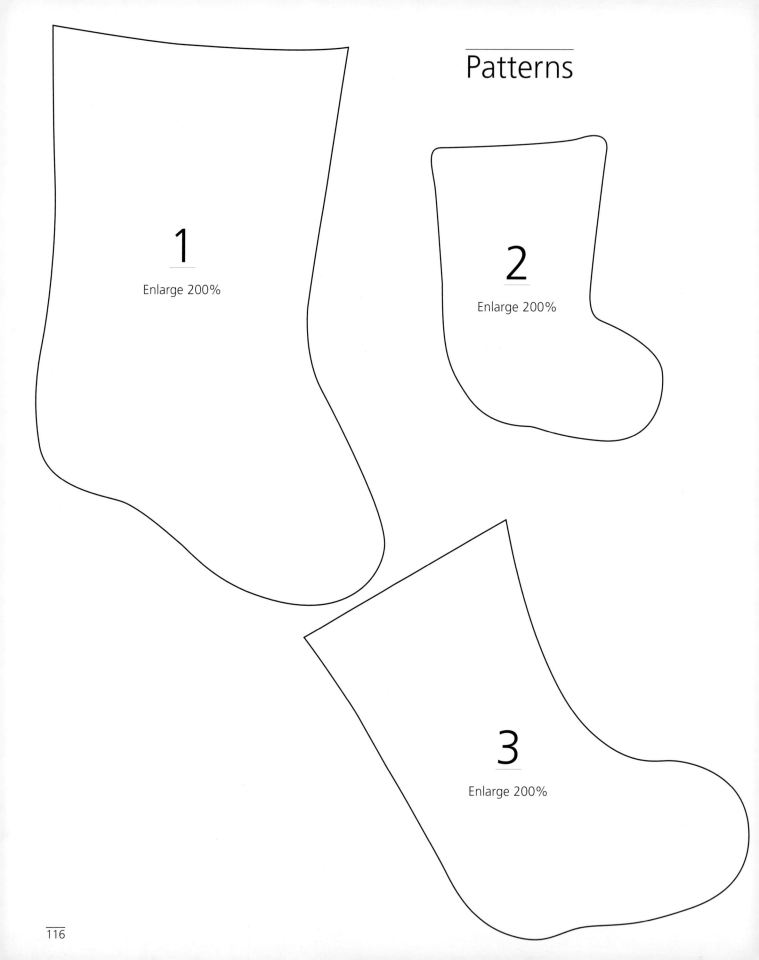

Patterns

1

Enlarge 200%

2

Enlarge 200%

3

Enlarge 200%

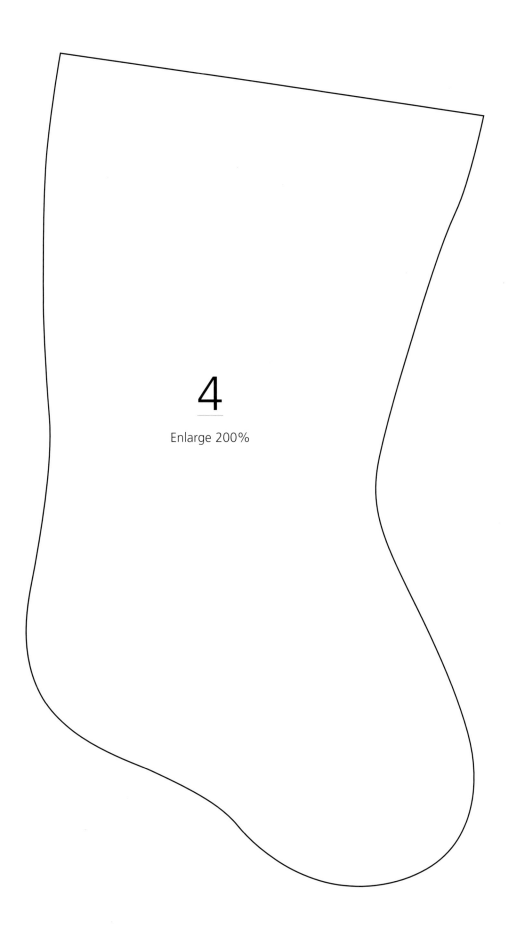

4

Enlarge 200%

5

Enlarge 200%

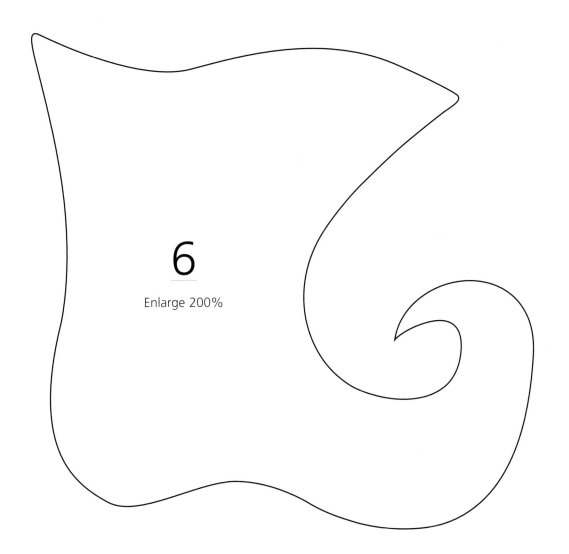

6

Enlarge 200%

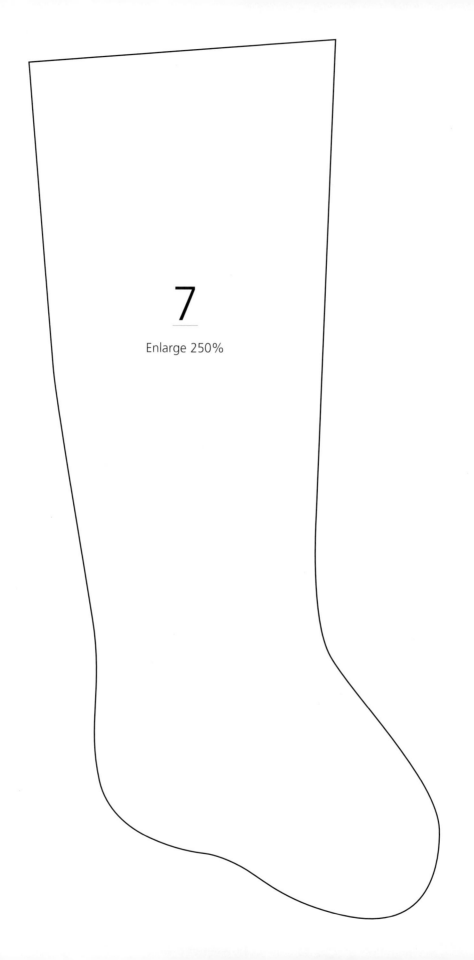

7

Enlarge 250%

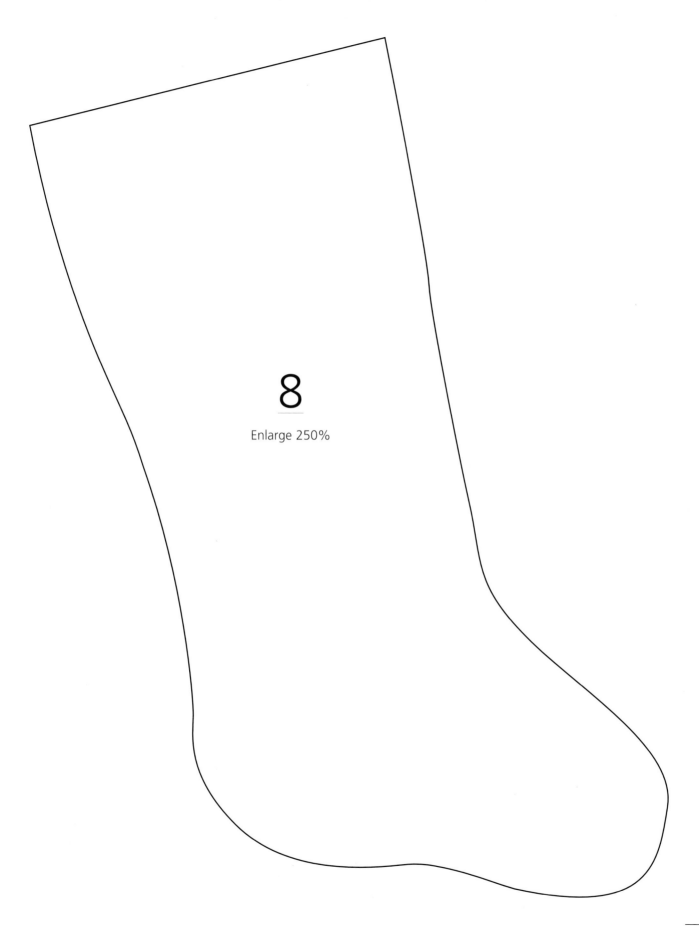

8

Enlarge 250%

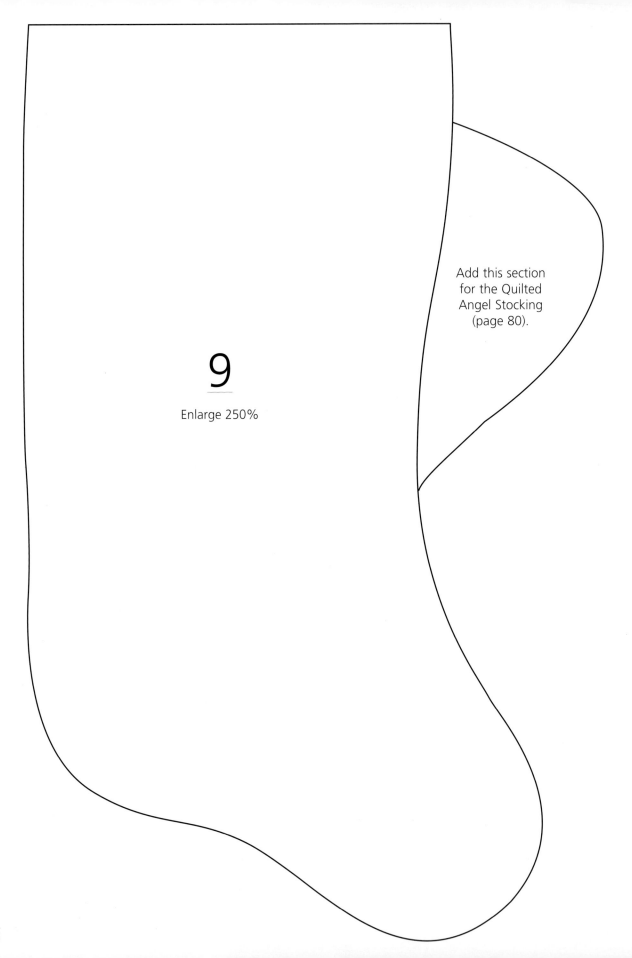

9

Enlarge 250%

Add this section
for the Quilted
Angel Stocking
(page 80).

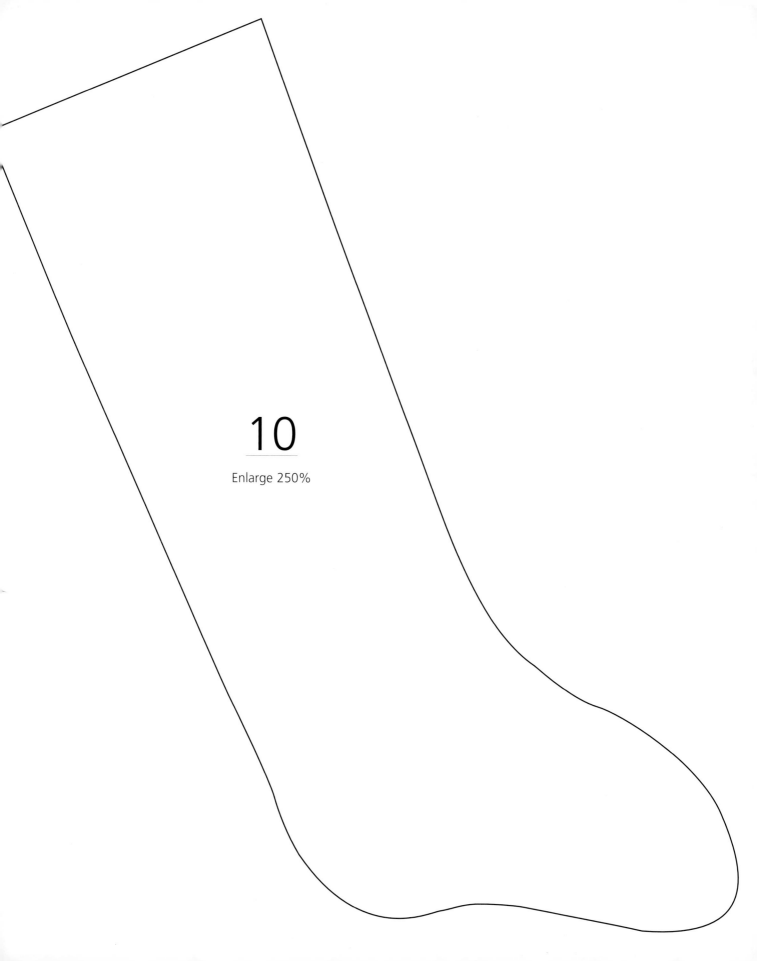

10

Enlarge 250%

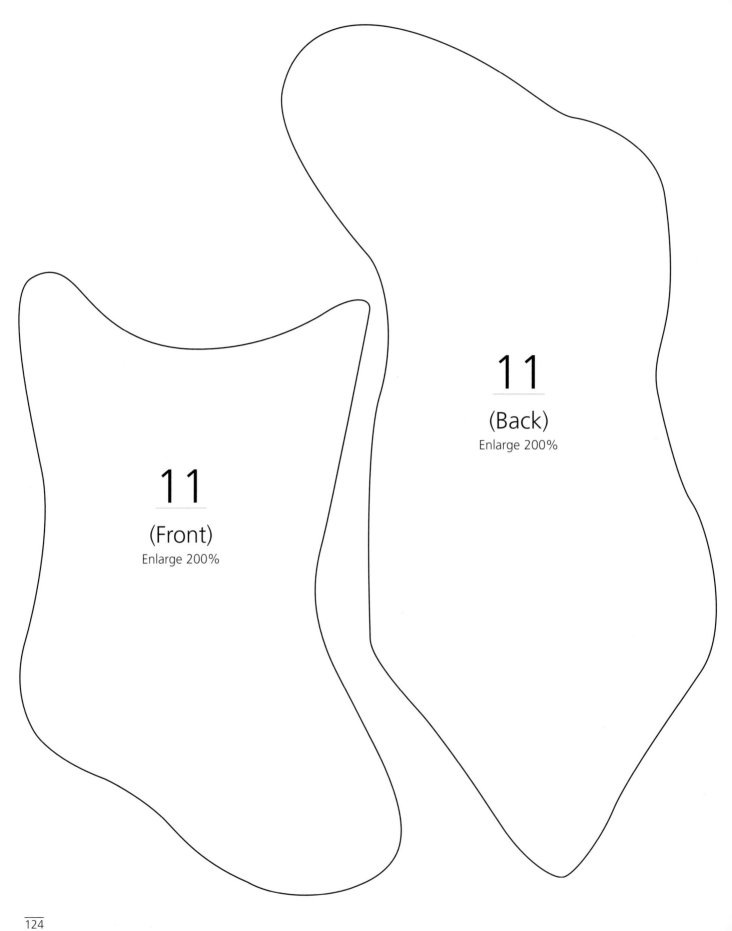

11

(Front)

Enlarge 200%

11

(Back)

Enlarge 200%

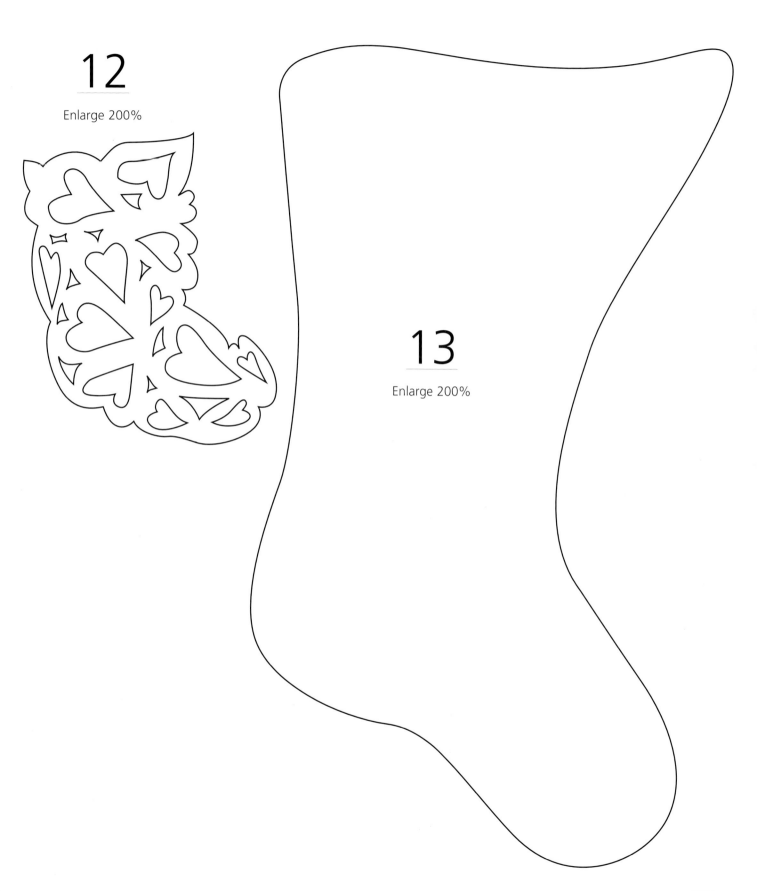

12

Enlarge 200%

13

Enlarge 200%

14

Enlarge 250%

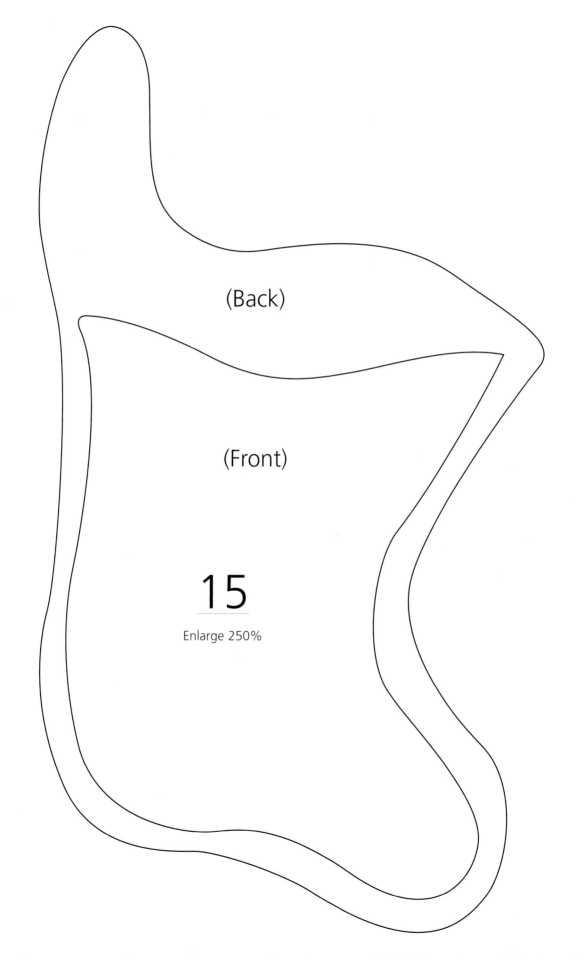

(Back)

(Front)

15

Enlarge 250%

Index